The Selected Works of Mahasweta Devi

Mahasweta Devi (b. 1926) is one of our foremost literary personalities, a prolific and best-selling author in Bengali of short fiction and novels; a deeply political social activist who has been working with and for tribals and marginalized communities like the landless labourers of eastern India for years; the editor of a quarterly, *Bortika*, in which the tribals and marginalized peoples themselves document grassroot level issues and trends; and a socio-political commentator whose articles have appeared regularly in the *Economic and Political Weekly*, *Frontier* and other journals.

Mahasweta Devi has made important contributions to literary and cultural studies in this country. Her empirical research into oral history as it lives in the cultures and memories of tribal communities was a first of its kind. Her powerful, haunting tales of exploitation and struggle have been seen as rich sites of feminist discourse by leading scholars. Her innovative use of language has expanded the conventional borders of Bengali literary expression. Standing as she does at the intersection of vital contemporary questions of politics, gender and class, she is a significant figure in the field of socially committed literature.

Recognizing this, we have conceived a publishing programme which encompasses a representational look at the complete Mahasweta: her novels, her short fiction, her children's stories, her plays, her activist prose writings. The series is an attempt to introduce her impressive body of work to a readership beyond Bengal; it is also an overdue recognition of the importance of her contribution to the literary and cultural history of our country.

The Selected Works of Mahasweta Devi

Mother of 1084
A Novel.Translated and introduced by
Samik Bandyopadhyay.

Breast Stories: Draupadi, Breast-Giver, Behind The Bodice
Translated with introductory essays by
Gayatri Chakravorty Spivak.

Five Plays: Mother of 1084, Aajir, Urvashi and Johnny, Bayen, Water
Adapted from her fiction by the author.
Translated and introduced by
Samik Bandyopadhyay.

Rudali: From Fiction to Performance
This volume consists of the story by Mahasweta Devi
and the play by Usha Ganguli.
Translated and introduced by Anjum Katyal.

Dust on the Road: The Activist Writings of Mahasweta Devi
A collection of prose pieces.
Introduced and translated by Maitreya Ghatak.

Bitter Soil
Palamau Stories by Mahasweta Devi.
Translated by Ipsita Chanda.
Introduced by the author.

Our Non-Veg Cow and Other Stories
Translated by Paramita Banerjee.
Introduced by Nabaneeta Dev Sen.

The Armenian Champa Tree
A Novella. Translated by
Nirmal Kanti Bhattacharjee.

Old Women
Two stories. Translated by
Gayatri Chakravorty Spivak.

RUDALI
From Fiction to Performance

MAHASWETA DEVI

USHA GANGULI

Translated with an introductory essay by
ANJUM KATYAL

CALCUTTA 1999

Translation and introductory material
© Seagull Books, 1997

First Printing 1997
Second Printing 1999

Cover image: Chittrovanu Mazumdar
Cover design: Naveen Kishore

ISBN 81 7046 138 3

The translator gratefully acknowledges the valuable responses
and suggestions provided by Samik Bandyopadhyay, Paramita
Banerjee and Kavita Panjabi to her essay 'The Metamorphosis of
"Rudali"'. She is also grateful to Samik Bandyopadhyay for his
careful reading of and suggestions for the translation of
Mahasweta Devi's 'Rudali'.

Published by Naveen Kishore,
Seagull Books Private Limited,
26 Circus Avenue, Calcutta 700 017, India

Printed in India by Laurens & Co
9 Crooked Lane, Calcutta 700 069

CONTENTS

The Metamorphosis
of 'Rudali'

'RUDALI', A PIECE OF SHORT FICTION in
Bengali by Mahasweta Devi, was adapted and produced as a
play in Hindi by Usha Ganguli of the Calcutta theatre group
Rangakarmee in December 1992. Since then it has had well
over a hundred shows, playing to packed houses, and has
drawn the attention of both critics and a theatre audience
more used to theatre in Bengali than Hindi. In both
incarnations of 'Rudali', it has been a woman auteur who has
wrought and then rewrought this text which revolves around
the life of a woman—the poor, lowcaste, Sanichari. Each
version is mediated by the differing purpose and agenda of its
respective author, resulting in strikingly different texts which
have one feature in common—they are perceived as woman-
intensive projects and received as feminist texts. This essay
sets out to study how and why the versions are different and
what the changes signify, leading to an analysis of how the
women auteurs propel their respective works towards very
different aims.

Since this essay will be using the conceptual term
'feminist' as a defining and categorizing word, it is important to establish just what it implies. At this juncture, in this
country, it is an overloaded, problematic term. Widely seen as

an imported western concept strongly identified with white bourgeois concerns and issues, the term is often aligned with elite urban intellectualism, and frequently seen as reductive or limiting. Ironically, this causes many liberated, activist, progressive women working with women's issues and rights in this country to shy away from the label of 'feminism' while practising it in their lives and work. Usha Ganguli expresses this paradox: 'I feel that I differ from the way people tend to use the term feminism. This term has nowadays become a fashionable one, and I don't believe in a particular brand of feminism. Therefore I don't want the play [*Rudali*] to be labelled as feminist. On the other hand, I believe in the liberation of women and their freedom, and I'm trying my best as a person, as a teacher and as a theatre worker to work towards that.'[1] Mahasweta Devi also shies away from being labelled 'feminist'. But if one detaches the word 'feminist' from specific class identifications, it can be used as a convenient umbrella term encompassing any person, element, process, form or production that promotes women's journey towards agency and empowerment—which is the general sense in which it has been used in this essay.

The first section of this essay deals with the original text, the short story 'Rudali' by Mahasweta Devi. It identifies the various aspects of the author's agenda—the multiple strands of which are all interwoven, logically implicated in each other—and then examines how this multi-strand agenda is worked through. The second part undertakes a detailed examination of the ways in which the playtext differs from the original, analysing the differences in signification that result.

I

In the short story, the text sees an evolution in the central character, Sanichari, who emerges at the end as better equipped to adapt, survive and manipulate the system—in other words, more empowered—than she is at the beginning. The implication is that familiarity with this one life will also familiarize us with the life of a community. The individual is historicized, not highlighted to the exclusion of context.

---

1. Interview with Usha Ganguli on 20 April, 1993.

Along with this agenda of historicization runs a harsh, powerful critique of an exploitative and repressive socio-economic and religious system. Confronting this the author positions the issue of survival, with an assertion of belief in the necessity for, and benefits of, community.

The author shows an awareness of a possible 'audience'—a literate, urban readership—in her agenda of desentimentalization, of a very deliberate stripping away of any romanticized view of these people, their lives and situation. She replaces the normative urban perception of the 'eternal' Indian village as unchanging, peaceful, nourished by tradition—a version of the romance of the pastorale—with her insider knowledge and subalternized perception of power structures and the corrupt ways of socially and economically dominant classes. Yet another important aspect of the work is the mode of presentation. In several ways, this work is anti-fiction: the author either subverts or ignores the conventions of a 'story' (although she utilizes certain elements of fictional narrative to realize her agenda), thus disrupting the easy receptivity to fiction ('it's just a story, after all'), and forcing her work onto the uneasy no-man's land between journalism and fiction that is most challenging for a bourgeois readership to negotiate.

Let us begin by examining the methods of historicization employed by the author. The opening sentences of 'Rudali' by Mahasweta Devi situate Sanichari in a socio-economic context, and firmly establish that Sanichari, who shares the condition of poverty with the other villagers, is one of a community: 'In Tahad village, ganjus and dushads were in the majority. Sanichari was a ganju by caste. *Like the other villagers, her life too was lived in desperate* poverty.'[1] The opening paragraph then carries on to state how her mother-in-law would often remark that, being born on an unlucky day of the week (Saturday or sanichar, hence her name, Sanichari), she was cursed, manhoos, doomed to suffer. But Sanichari can't see that those born on so-called 'lucky' days have an easier time of it. It's not fate, not a question of being born on this or that day. It's an economic condition. The very first paragraph thus

---

1. Mahasweta Devi, 'Rudali' in *Nairitey Megh* (Calcutta: Karuna Prakashani, 1980). Emphasis added. This and all subsequent quotes from this text are from my translation, in this volume.

underscores the tension between the 'givens' of fate/karma and the historicity of a politically and economically construct-ed situation, challenging the concept of a 'natural' order. Right from the beginning, therefore, the story places the central character in her historical situation, provides a socio-economic context and emphasizes that her problems are common to her class, caste and gender.

Sanichari is not individuated through a description of her appearance, her clothes, mannerisms, habits of speech—when she speaks, she uses the same dialect, sounds like any of the other villagers of her class. The author is not interested in sculpting a three-dimensional portrait of a rounded 'character' through psychological and physical description. In fact, the only time the author describes her is when she meets up with her childhood playmate Bikhni, and then the purpose of the descriptive passage is to establish similarity, that she is the same in appearance as her friend and the other women of their class.

This insistence on embedding Sanichari in the broader context continues through the text in various other ways. Direct authorial statements link her story to a larger discourse of struggle and exploitation. ('In this village everyone is unhappy. They understand suffering.') There is a continuous suturing of her private life to the socio-economic situation, to history. 'When her mother-in-law died, Sanichari didn't cry. At the time, her husband and his brother, both the old woman's sons, were in jail because of malik-mahajan Ramavatar Singh. Enraged at the loss of some wheat, he had all the young dushad and ganju males of the village locked up.' When her brother- and sister-in-law die, she is unable to weep because she is tense over the fact that Ramavatar is trying to have all the dushads and ganjus evicted from the village. Ramavatar's oppression is a constant presence. He embodies a system which dehumanizes, brutalizes, invading the most private space of an individual, the emotions, so that even grief is distorted in the desperate struggle for survival. Grief is turned into a commodity, and mourning is labour. If sorrow is controlled by the malik-mahajan, tears can be used as a produce, a source of earning by professional mourners. (In fact, this commodification of grief is shown first as a characteristic of the malik-mahajan's social class: when there is a death in their families, they have to hire rudalis to mourn for them, so as to enhance their prestige; since this market exists, the outcast and marginalized can supply their skilled labour to service it.)

If we look at all the 'events' in Sanichari's life as shown in the text, we find a direct connection between the personal event and the exploitative system. Every death is mediated by the religious demands that follow for rituals which further impoverish the already poor. Sanichari's husband dies of cholera after drinking the contaminated and putrid 'sanctified' milk donated to the Shiva idol by the rich. She is made to pay twice over for ritual offerings. The second time, in order to appease the local village priest—who is also Ramavatar Singh's family priest—she is forced into indebtedness to Ramavatar.

Every loss she suffers is because of the dire poverty, the constricted life, the total lack of hope of any change or improvement—her daughter-in-law Parbatia and her grandson Haroa both leave because they refuse to submit to the harsh conditions, even though their options are prostitution and the insecurities of a wandering life. Her son Budhua contracts tuberculosis while hauling sacks of wheat for Ramavatar's son Lachman Singh. When her grandson comes of age, she takes him to Lachman Singh for a job. There is no other source of employment. Oppression is hereditary, for both the exploiter and the exploited.

The author also uses more overt methods of historicization, such as a subaltern view of local politics and the hypocrisy of the privileged classes. Although offered also by the other characters, this criticism is usually spoken by Dulan, who is acknowledged by members of his community as a knowing one ('Come, let's go to see Dulan. He's a crafty old rogue, but he has a sharp mind. He's sure to show us a way,' says Sanichari). In addition, such critique is often expressed in the narrator's voice. For example, the episode in which Lachman Singh makes his appearance beside the murdered corpse of his kinsman Bhairab Singh (p.67–68) is recounted by the narrating agent, focalized through the observing village community. This entire passage employs a 'no comment' technique, using an ostensibly objective 'reporting' mode to expose the hypocrisy and corruption of 'the masters.' In a single passage the author spotlights their criminality, greed, vicious discrimination against the lower

castes, power to manipulate police and investigative proce-
dures, infighting, and the determination with which they
close class ranks in the face of a possible threat.

Yet another way of historicizing the text is by the
insertion of passages of oral history, told by one character to
another, passages which explain present conditions and
analyse how they are caused. Usually the speaker is Dulan.
There is one passage in particular which exemplifies this
method, in which Dulan tells them about their local history.
'There is no revolution without memory.'[1] Dulan helps keep
memory alive, reminding them of a past in which they
organized themselves in resistance, a past of heroism and
courage. 'The tale Dulan told them was very significant; it
explained clearly how the ruthless Rajputs infiltrated this
remote area of tribals and from zamindars gradually built
themselves up to the status of jotedar/moneylenders and
established themselves as the masters of the area.' He talks to
them about the militant rebel tribal leaders Harda and Donka
Munda, of tribal uprisings brutally repressed by the Rajput
soldiers sent by the raja of Chhotanagpur, who burned entire
villages and murdered the innocent, of how the Rajput
sardars were told by the raja to claim as much land as was
covered by throwing their swords in the air, of how nowadays
the Rajputs increase their land not by throwing swords but by
shooting bullets at people and flinging flaming torches at
settlements.

> There may be litigations and illwill between the
> maliks, but they have certain things in common. Except
> for salt, kerosene and postcards, they don't need to buy
> anything. They have elephants, horses, livestock,
> illegitimate children, kept women, venereal disease
> and a philosophy that he who owns the gun owns the
> land. They all worship household deities who repay
> them amply—after all, in the name of the deities they
> hold acres which are exempt from taxes and reforms.

He is politicizing them; and coming from one of them, this
analysis carries greater impact. Similarly he analyses for
Bikhni, Sanichari and his wife how the malik-mahajans

---

1. Henrich Muller, 'A Letter to Robert Wilson' in *Explosion of Memory* (New
York: PAJ Publications, 1989), p.153.

create prostitutes by keeping women and then casting them off, thereby forcing them into the marketplace. Whores are not a separate caste, as they believe, merely poor women like them who are forced to earn a living. He establishes that the exploitation' of the poor by the rich takes many forms, that the prostitutes too are victims, and should not be treated like outcasts and untouchables. He proposes solidarity rather than prejudice.

The entire text is a critique of the socio-economic and religious systems, and the nexus between them. By showing the dire poverty of the villagers, the ways in which they are exploited, the burden of ritualized religion, the absolute power of the malik-mahajans, and the corruption within the privileged classes, the author constructs a powerful indictment. This indictment is spoken by the villagers, or through direct authorial addresses placed throughout the text, which act almost as a refrain: 'Everything in this life is a battle.' The preoccupation with earning enough to subsist on, the references to getting by on a half-empty stomach, the hard struggle to produce food, the imposed austerity with even little indulgences like bangles or a comb appearing to be impossible dreams, are juxtaposed against frequent references to the wanton way in which the rich spend money on funerary ceremonies. 'For them, nothing has ever come easy. Just the daily struggle for a little maize gruel and salt is exhausting. Through motherhood and widowhood they're tied to the moneylender. While those people spend huge sums of money on death ceremonies, just to gain prestige'; or 'When someone died in a malik-mahajan household, the amount of money spent on the death ceremony immediately raised the prestige of the family . . . The price for this is paid by the dushads, dhobis, ganjus and kols, from the hides of whom the overlords extracted the sums they had overspent.' Sanichari, who borrows a meagre .Rs 20 for her husband's shradh, has to repay Rs 50 through bonded labour over the next five years, while thousands of rupees are carelessly spent on the lavish shradhs of her masters. Malik-mahajans like Ramavatar Singh, and later his son Lachman Singh, are shown as controlling and influencing almost every aspect of the lives of the lowercaste villagers. Not only can they have the men locked up whenever they feel like it, they can use and discard the women and extract years of unpaid labour as repayment for small debts.

Confronting this is the cynical contempt of the villagers, who are shown as cherishing no illusions about the greed, miserliness or moral bankruptcy of their 'masters', though they are forced to submit to their power. They are repressed, but not colonized. Dulan is particularly outspoken about the warped ways of the upper classes: after a scathing account of how Nathuni Singh, who owes all his wealth to his mother, is doing nothing to treat her, he adds, 'He's not willing to spend a paisa on trying to cure her, but plans to spend thirty thousand on her funeral!' Even Sanichari says, 'These people can't summon up tears even at the death of their own brothers and fathers . . . Do you know that Gangadhar Singh . . . was stingy enough to use dalda instead of pure ghee on the funeral pyre of his uncle?' The sharply observant eyes of the subaltern keep the privileged in perspective.

Paralleling the economic stranglehold of the malik-mahajans is the social oppression of a religious system which controls through fear and superstition. Not once, throughout the story, is religion shown as offering solace or succour. On the contrary, religion further impoverishes and enslaves, causing indebtedness through its web of demands and obligations. All one sees of religion is superstition and ritual. When Sanichari's mother-in-law dies, at night, in the pouring rain, Sanichari is hard pressed to carry out the necessary rituals before daybreak, with no grain in the house, and no menfolk to help lay out the body. When Sanichari's brother- and sister-in-law die, 'There was no crying over those deaths either. Was one to weep or to worry about how to burn the corpses and feed the neighbours cheaply at the shradh?' When her husband dies, she has barely had time to register the fact when the panda of the Shiva temple at Tohri demands that she make ritual offerings before returning to her village. Even a spartan offering of sand and sattu (gram flour) costs her a precious rupee and a quarter. And once she returns to her village, Mohanlal, the priest of Ramavatar's presiding deity, scoffs—'Can a Tohri brahman know how a Tahad villager's kriya is done?' To think that these are neighbouring villages! He is deeply offended; to appease him she has to repeat the offerings—and to afford this, she is forced into debt to Ramavatar. A perfect example of how religious and economic exploitation reinforce and strengthen one another.

It is not as if religious superstition does not apply to the rich—they are as bound by rules and regulations, and as controlled by fear. The difference is that they can afford it, and even benefit by it financially, as Dulan points out when he talks about tax benefits from acres of land dedicated to family deities. The author also shows how the rich manipulate religion to their own ends—for example, Gambhir Singh pays astrologers and pandits to find out that his only sin has been that of striking a pregnant cow as a boy.

Set against this exploitative system is the issue of survival. 'Rudali is about . . . "how to survive" . . . "bread and mouth". It is very important in my story. The whole system is exposed through this,' says Mahasweta Devi.[1] The text explicates the various strategies of survival employed by the subaltern individually and as a community.

A major narrative tool used to this end is her construct of the character of Dulan. He embodies the resistant will, the sharp intelligence, the irreverence, the cynicism, and the cunning that the subaltern uses to subvert the total control of the masters. He is also, as we have seen, the oral narrator of their history, the one who constantly questions authority and teaches the others to be critical of it. It is Dulan who at every stage contributes to the growing empowerment of Sanichari, who shows her how to adapt and cope. The first time we see Dulan is illustrative of this (p.57). This is also the first real dialogue in the text which is between peers, presented directly and not through a narrative agent, the first time we hear the characters speak in their 'own' voices. This highlights the significance of the interchange. Dulan's intervention is positive. He succeeds in diverting her mind from helpless despair (mourning her fate, her dead husband) to a realization that actually she's angry about the unfairness of her situation—and then he presents her with a survival strategy, a way of turning the situation around so that she is using the system instead of just being used by it.

At every stressful juncture of her life, Dulan intervenes to advise, help, educate, enlighten. Mahasweta Devi refuses to foreground the gender issue vis-a-vis community relations; in the process she bypasses even a hint of patriarchy. That Dulan

1 Interview with Mahasweta Devi in Calcutta on 26.5.93.

might be perceived as a male playing mentor and guide to helpless females is not a concern of the author's; and as a result Dulan and Sanichari interact as peers, unselfconsciously free from any hint of asymmetry in their relationship. When her son Budhua dies and she's deserted by her daughter-in-law, with an infant grandson to bring up, Dulan gets her a job repairing the railway line. When Bikhni's money runs out, they go to Dulan for advice. He suggests that they hire themselves out as rudalis. He accompanies them and negotiates on their behalf, making sure that they get a good deal. (Even the manner in which he does this is telling. He knows exactly how much has been budgeted for the funerary expenses and reveals this to the accounts-keeper who is obliged to accept his terms, wondering how Dulan knows so much about inside matters. Knowledge, information, is power. Dulan, who functions with a total absence of subservience or servility, can apply pressure precisely because knowledge has given him this power. He becomes, therefore, a threat to his so-called superiors.) Once the two women execute this job successfully, he gives them tips on how to keep themselves informed about potential jobs by keeping an ear open on trips to the marketplace. He tells them to offer an additional service—extra rudalis garnered from the whore bazaar. Towards the end of the story, when Sanichari is faced with the knowledge that she is on her own now that Bikhni is dead, she goes to Dulan once again for advice; and their conversation is very significant, since it leads directly to Sanichari's shift in self-image from that of helpless victim to empowerment and agency.

> Dulan . . . grasped the gravity of the situation at once, said, look, Budhua's ma. It's wrong to give up one's land, and your profession of funeral wailing is like your land, you mustn't give it up.'

He draws a direct equation between professional mourning and physical labour. In fact, he had earlier suggested to Sanichari that, just as the coalminers had a union, they should form a union of rudalis and whores, of which she could be president. Just this one comment exposes how sophisticated his understanding of labour relationships is: he fully appreciates that rudalis are professionals in the same way that the organized labour sector is. He says that just as, when her husband died, she took over his work in the malik's fields, she must take over Bikhni's work, which means interacting with the prostitutes in Tohri. He intuits that she is embarrassed by her daughter-in-law's presence in the Tohri randipatti (whores' quarter), and urges her to involve Parbatia as well. Dulan's reasoning, his insistence that the prostitutes are victims just like themselves, breaks down Sanichari's resistance—rooted in convention—to the idea that her own daughter-in-law is now a prostitute. He opens up an avenue by which she can accept her. One worry remains in Sanichari's mind—'Won't the village speak ill of me?' Dulan laughs bitterly, 'What one is forced to do to feed oneself is never considered wrong.' She has always put a premium on community support and approval; Dulan's encouragement reassures her, and thereafter the Sanichari we see is confident, uninhibited, canny.

Throughout, Dulan's is the voice stripping away sentimentality and blind prejudice in favour of adaptation and rational argument. His is the voice that criticizes, accuses and condemns the upper classes, highlights their moral corruption, greed and hypocrisy. By doing so he is helping maintain a critical perspective on the system, and in effect politicizing the community. He refuses to believe or allow them to believe that there is anything ordained or natural about their situation. 'Every social group coming into existence on the original terrain of an essential function in the world of economic production, creates together with itself, organically, one or more strata of intellectuals which give it homogeneity and an awareness of its own function not only in the economic but also in the social and political fields,' says Gramsci.[1] The figure of Dulan ganju is configured as just such an 'organic intellectual'.

It is important to note the way in which Dulan communicates. He speaks as one of the villagers—the same dialect, no sense of 'talking down'—and the women, while valuing his sharp mind, aren't especially in awe of him. In fact his acerbic wife cuts in with sharp comments while he talks. There is no aura of authority surrounding him, and he does nothing to court it. Neither is everything he says accepted

---

1. Antonio Gramsci, *Selections from Prison Notebooks* (Lawrence and Wishart, London, 1991), p. 5

unquestioningly. Sanichari, despite his persuasive analysis, remains unclear about how and why women become prostitutes; but that doesn't prevent her from following his practical advice. He is not positioned as a leader in any formal sense. Dulan is a fellow villager. No more, no less. Sidestepping gendered hierarchy and formalized patriarchal authority, the author stresses community.

She never passes up a chance to emphasize the value and necessity of community, partnership, fraternity and sisterhood as essential survival aids. She does this through direct statements: 'There are some debts that can never be repaid . . . If her fellow-villagers had not rallied around in this manner, would Sanichari have survived?' She is careful to show up the clan and class solidarity among the rich when facing a challenge, either from the lower classes or the police—not only does Dulan comment on it, Lachman Singh's words on the occasion of Bhairab Singh's murder make it explicit. There may be bitter infighting amongst them over land and riches, but they band together to present a united front when threatened from without. If community can be a tool of offence and defence for the exploiters, it has to be a form of protection and strength for the exploited.

After Budhua's death, when Sanichari finds herself totally alone, she experiences the support and bonding a community can offer. She is having a hard time tending to her infant grandson, who won't stop crying. One day Dulan's wife comes by and picks up the baby, stating matter-of-factly that her daughter-in-law, who is nursing, will breastfeed this child along with her own. She also brings Sanichari news of a job which can help her earn some money: perfect examples of networking, solidarity, communal mothering—all of this in a matter-of-fact, down-to-earth manner, with no nuance of condescension or charity.

Dulan and his family look out for her, and Parbhu ganju comes up with an offer to shift her hut into his own compound. Natua dushad sells her vegetables for her in the market. In addition there is sensitivity over topics which could be painful or embarrassing ('No one mentioned that Budhua's wife had become a whore')—none of the jeering or attempt to enjoy another's discomfiture which is the clichéd representation of how neighbours, especially women, react when a scandal occurs.

Sanichari herself is shown as being fully aware of how essential to survival community is. Reflecting on her bahu's behaviour she thinks, 'In order to survive, the poor and oppressed need the support of the other poor and oppressed. Without that support, it is impossible to live in the village even on milk and ghee provided by the malik.' The author does not show any act of meanness or exploitation between the villagers, neither between women, nor between men and women. (The only exceptions to this are Sanichari's mother-in-law who, however, is hardly a presence, since she dies in the second paragraph; and the restless bahu who deserts her child and runs away—and even that 'treachery' is resolved by Sanichari's understanding and her inclusion at the end.) But as for the malik-mahajans, the text bristles with references to their veniality and callousness, showing them killing, cheating and betraying close relatives for monetary gain.

Amongst the poor all the exploitation is vertical. Horizontally, the author posits class solidarity as the norm. As part of this agenda, she shows men and women of the lower classes/castes as helpful and supportive of each other. Dulan is a major example of this at the level of community; and at the level of the family, where the husband, father or household head are commonly oppressors of the women, the author presents an alternative picture. Sanichari and her husband are shown as partners, both working equally hard, but together, for home and livelihood. She leaves her six-year-old son at home and goes to the malik's estate where she chops wood, fetches fodder for the cattle, and at harvest season works shoulder to shoulder with her husband. Together the two of them erect a hut on the piece of land they have inherited after the death of her brother-in-law. She draws decorative pictures on the walls, he plans a vegetable patch in their courtyard, she arranges to rear one of the malkin's (mistress's) calves.

In an unusual reversal of the normative male-family-member type, Sanichari's son Budhua is shown as sensitive, thoughtful, gentle, caring, both towards his mother and his wife, though the two are not compatible. He understands both these very different women and is capable of being compassionate and not judgemental. There is a detailed description of how Budhua laboured to develop the vegetable patch in their courtyard, which also serves to emphasize the hard labour necessary to produce food. Sanichari, delighted, comments on how his father had wanted a vegetable patch just like this: men as householders.

The author underscores Budhua's sensitivity, first towards his mother, whose anger at his wife he understands, and with whom he expresses solidarity ('How is she to know, ma, how you and I have struggled to build this little household—') and then towards his wife's restlessness and longing for more than their stringent circumstances can offer. Instead of merely using his authority as husband and male to forbid her leaving home, he strives to find a solution, a way of keeping her occupied, providing her with something to do and a means of earning a little extra to indulge her unappeased appetite. To this end, he slaves over the vegetable patch, so that selling vegetables in the market will provide her with both occupation and some additional income. When his mother expresses her uneasiness at the freedom this allows her, offering to go to market in her stead, he makes a telling reply: 'No, ma. When you and I slogged in the fields, she stayed at home. Did she ever cook, clean, fetch water?' He is fully aware of his wife's limitations, yet does not condemn her by what, after all, are the normative standards of expectation of a wife's duties. Moreover, he speaks up to prevent his mother from condemning her too harshly.

So valued is this gentle son by his mother that when it comes to the experience of losing him, the entire language of the text alters. The dry, staccato statements which describe the death of Sanichari's husband are replaced by a more repetitive, intense, emotional rhythm. Throughout this passage the narrative agency identifies closely with Sanichari's emotional state:

> That day—not just that day, for several days before that—Budhua's condition had worsened. The *vaid's* medicine was not working. Sanichari asked her to stay with Budhua. She herself went, running all the way she went, to ask the *vaid* for some other medicine. She went even though she knew that no medicine could help him now.

The loss of Budhua is the loss of a sympathetic, supportive, caring companion. Sanichari cannot imagine a life without him:

> She couldn't remember a time when he wasn't there

with her. While she slaved in the malik-mahajan's
fields, he would clean the house and fetch water from
the river. He would take the grains of wheat and corn
scavenged from the dusty fields, and wash them clean
in the river. Gentle, quiet, understanding—the son of a
suffering mother. How could she accept that she would
never again have to warm water for him at night, or
rub him down . . .

The author balances this close relationship with Bikhni's sad
tale of a selfish son who walks out on his mother for a better
life as a live-in son-in-law, taking the cows which are his
mother's only means of livelihood. All sons and husbands
may not be as caring as Budhua, but by detailing a positive
relationship between male and female members of a family
the author opens up a space for the possibility of such supportive
relationships.

The relationship between Sanichari and Bikhni,
childhood playmates who rediscover each other as ageing,
lonely women and decide to team up, is the major statement
of bonding and support within a community made in the text.
These women are not related, they have only their
circumstances in common—both have been abandoned by
members of their family, who could have provided them with
support in their old age. Both are poor, struggling to find
means of survival. By pairing up they provide each other with
company, and pool their resources to ensure a degree of
economic stability. The relationship between the two of them
will be taken up in detail later in this paper.

Mahasweta Devi expands the notion of community to
include the prostitutes, women who are traditionally seen as
outside community, or as forming an outcast, separate
community of their own. We see women from the village
who have become prostitutes—they have mothers and families
within the village community, histories which locate them
in the community. Some have been used by the malik-
mahajans and then discarded; some have mothers who were
kept women and are forced into prostitution in their turn;
others become prostitutes because they have run away from
home, looking for better options to the humdrum,
circumscribed existence their poverty and social class locks
them into. Dulan explains at some length the socio-economic

causes that have led to their becoming prostitutes, and accuses the malik-mahajans of being responsible. He undoes the common belief that the prostitutes are 'other', and establishes that they are poor working women trying to fill their stomachs like everyone else, as much victims of exploitation as themselves. He encourages Sanichari and Bikhni to work with them, to take them into the community. Parbatia is a good example of the way in which the text resolves the issue of prostitutes. She escapes from a severely circumscribed, poverty-ridden existence, leaving behind all duties and responsibilities—even her infant son—driven by a hunger and need in excess of what her daily life can offer. She runs off with a wandering medicineman, who entices her with promises of places to see, exotic marvels like nautanki (dance) shows, cinemas and circuses and daily treats of puri-kachuri. In a few years she is back, a down-on-her-luck prostitute in Tohri. At the end of the story, she is drawn back into the fold by her erstwhile mother-in-law, who invites her to join the community of rudalis. And the text closes on this note, with Sanichari organizing and training the prostitutes into a group. They are gathered into the space of the narrative, included.

Mahasweta Devi is firm in rejecting the idea that this text could be especially identified with women in any way, since gender is subsumed into the discourse of class. To emphasize the former at the expense of the latter is a 'denial of history as she sees it'.[1] 'For you it may be important that this story is written by a woman . . . another woman has adapted it into a play . . . But I think that a writer has written the story, a director has adapted it into a play. *It is not very important to me whether it was done by a woman or not . . . I write as a writer, not as a woman.* . . When I write I never think of myself as a woman. I have written a story called *Chetty Munda and His Arrow* which is about a tribal man. *Aranyer Adhikar* is about male tribals. So what? These are stories of people's struggle, their confrontation with the system . . . *I look at the class, not at the gender problem.* Take a story like *Ganesh Mahima* —it is about a woman. But I have written it from the class point of view. In 'Rudali' you have a character like Dulan who

---

1. Comment by Samik Bandyopadhyay during the interview with Mahasweta Devi on 26.5.93.

knows how to use the system. In my stories men and women alike belong to different classes.'[1]

There is no doubt that the text does privilege class and community over women's issues in isolation. And yet it has special significance when read as a feminist text. The common accusation made by those who privilege a cross-class gender perspective to those who position gender issues within those of class is that the woman's perspective tends to get marginalized or elided over in the 'general' interest of the class. Perhaps because Mahasweta Devi writes from a 'class point of view' but is herself a woman, there is no sign of this in her text, not even through slippages. In fact, her text shows us that gender and class need not be viewed as polarities; that one's discourse can be informed by class and simultaneously be gendered. One political stance need not rule out the other.[2]

In what ways is this an enabling feminist text? Firstly, 'Rudali' traces, as mentioned above, Sanichari's growing empowerment, which is helped by Bikhni's more open and adaptive attitude to new ideas and opportunities. The Sanichari we encounter at the end of the story—outgoing, shrewd, manipulative—is very different from the stoic, long-suffering but repressed woman we see earlier. The trajectory of the central character is towards agency. Secondly, 'Rudali' highlights bonding between women. There is the subtly nuanced closeness between Sanichari and Bikhni which is especially poignant, as such friendships are rarely detailed in literature. Accounts of girlhood friendships, yes, even bonding between young women, and of course, close relationships between boys and men, abound—but it is very rare, particularly in Indian literature, to come across an intimate relationship between two older women treated with such sensitive, affectionate (but totally unsentimental) tenderness. There is also the almost casual but very vital support offered each other by neighbouring women when it comes to breast-feeding a motherless baby, helping out by cooking a meal or sharing surplus food. (Interestingly, this kind of networking is not shown as occurring between women of the higher classes. Amongst the wives of the malik-mahajans we see

---

1. Interview with Mahasweta Devi on 26.5.93. Emphasis mine.
2. The development of this thought to its present emphasis comes from Paramita Banerjee.

mutual jealousy, spiteful gossip and one-upmanship, as well as an internalization of class values and attitudes such as pride in displays of wealth and power.) Thirdly, the author also shows up how women across class lines remain objects of similar kinds of discrimination and social prejudice—there is the sequence in which Nathuni's middle wife complains to Sanichari about how she is looked down upon and denied respect because she is the mother of a girl, whereas her co-wives, by giving birth to sons, have secured their privileged positions. This social attitude, widely internalized by the women, which holds a woman solely responsible for all so-called ills and misfortunes (such as the lack of sons and heirs) echoes Sanichari's mother-in-law's accusations that it was unlucky, accursed Sanichari who was to blame for all the hardship in their family. The irony here, of course, is that the upper-class women may feel themselves privileged, but are still bound by the same social and cultural prejudices that affect the poorer women. Fourthly, there are passages of a rare and particular sensitivity to the women characters—for example, the sequence where Sanichari is brooding over her son's terminal illness. She feels as if the flames of the funeral pyre are burning her up inside. She can see that he is going to die, and realizes that her dreams of living to a peaceful old age in the bosom of her family, surrounded by grand-children, will not be fulfilled. Even her more modest dreams have never been realized. She had wanted to buy a wooden comb for her hair, to wear bangles for a full year—neither of these dreams had materialized. 'With time, her dreams had changed shape.' Earlier they were more girlish: dressing up, romance. Then, more domestic and matronly—her family well settled, earning well, enough to eat, sitting in the winter sun sharing a bowl of gud and sattu with her grandson—'had this last dream been over-ambitious? Had she sinned by wanting too much?' (Even aspiration can be a sin. Know your place. Keep in your place.) In just a few lines the author poignantly conveys the journey from girlhood through young womanhood to middle age, with its shifting aspirations and priorities, through the dreams of this woman who had longed for so little and got even less. Another instance of this sensitivity to a woman's psychology is the passage in which the author describes Bikhni's love of domesticity: 'Bikhni loved housework. Within a couple of days, she had put a fresh coat of mud and dung on the floor of the house and compound, washed Sanichari's and her own clothes thoroughly, aired all the mats and quilts . . . ' Here ordinary household chores get transformed, so that they become both a source and an expression of positive energy and confidence. The household is a domain where the woman can have control, when there is no dominant male. Being in charge is a good feeling, and domesticity allows Bikhni to relish it. And finally, although Mahasweta Devi shrugs off the gendered metaphor of the rudali by saying that this particular profession just happens to be open only to women, she has created a powerful and complex symbol—rich in ironies—in the closing image of her text: an organized band of women, comprised of the marginalized and outcast, intervening to subvert the solemn hypocrisy of an occasion which is a metonymy for a patriarchal, exploitative system. Turning a casual, part-time occupation into an organized profession for marginalized women is a fictional construct.[1] What the author is, in effect, doing, is transforming a woman-intensive casual labour sector into an organized sector—a conceptual twist significant in feminist terms, in terms of financial agency.

And now for a closer look at the relationship between Sanichari and Bikhni, which, like the character of Dulan, is a major fictional strategy used by the author to inflect a whole gamut of signification. By the time Sanichari comes upon Bikhni by chance at a local mela, she has already lost every member of her family: her husband, her son, her daughter-in-law and her grandson, who has run away. In fact, the text explicitly states that 'when she had given up hope of recovering Haroa, suddenly she met Bikhni.' At this point, she is a woman shorn of all roles—no-one's daughter, wife, mother, mother-in-law or grandmother. She is free of all other ties and relationships, as is Bikhni, who has been abandoned by her son, and has left home with no plans and nowhere to go. Untethered thus from the ties of family and all that family imposes by way of roles, duties and self-imaging, Sanichari and Bikhni are in a highly unusual situation for Indian women, one that allows them to bond a

---

1. This insight was expressed by Samik Bandyopadhyay in his valuable response to an early draft of this paper.

friendship and partnership which, free from preconceptions and societal norms, can, in a sense, invent itself. Socially and financially they are equals; both are equally without family, equally abandoned: on the basis of their common situation they construct their companionship. Once again the author turns disability into an enabling force.

This meeting between long-lost playmates has all the potential of a highly sentimental, emotionally charged reunion. In this author's relentlessly anti-sentimental hands it is anything but. To begin with, they bump into each other by accident and, both being tough old women, launch into a mutually satisfying exchange of insults. When, recognizing each other, they sit under the shade of a tree to chat and catch up, they first check each other out, to see if life has treated the other any better—and relax in the knowledge that they're both equally badly off. As equals, they can be friends, trade stories of hardship and betrayal, without any attempt to save face or put up a front. They bring each other up to date. Compared to Sanichari, Bikhni is more devil-may-care, more rebellious. When her son refused to help her pay off the debt she had incurred in order to arrange his marriage, and cut off her means of livelihood by taking away her cows, she decamped with their goats, sold them, and was prepared to survive by begging at railway stations if necessary. This bold readiness to break out of the restrictions imposed on women like them by religious and social custom gradually rubs off on Sanichari. Later, when Dulan suggests that they become rudalis, Bikhni takes to the idea immediately, and her willing acceptance helps Sanichari to get used to it. When she asks, 'Won't there be talk in the village?' Bikhni dismissively replies, 'So let them talk!' When they need reinforcements and Dulan suggests bringing in the prostitutes from Tohri, it is once again Bikhni who readily agrees to go and negotiate with them, while Sanichari demurs, worried about what the village will say. Dulan and Bikhni are equally instrumental in the gradual empowerment of Sanichari. By the end of the story she has taken on Bikhni's assertive manner.

Sanichari invites Bikhni to share her little house. It will be company for her, a place for Bikhni to stay. In response, Bikhni offers her nest-egg: twenty rupees. They are pooling resources, forming an economic unit radically different from the traditional family unit. This goes against the norm—the village community is surprised at the way Bikhni settles down and becomes part of their life: 'Bikhni surprised everyone. She didn't go to visit her son even once.' After all, women belong in families. This twosome proves that community coheres irrespective of family and blood ties—Sanichari and Bikhni are an example of this: 'People who come from far away, strangers, can become as close as one's own kin. Like the bark of one tree grafted on to another.'

The author devotes much of the text to tracing their evolution into a professional team. Bikhni would visit the markets and bazaars, the shops near the bus-stop. She would bring news of who was dying in which rich household. The two of them would wrap their black cloth round themselves and knot a snack into their anchals. They would present themselves at the 'big house' and briskly lay down their terms, negotiating directly with the gomastha (accounts keeper), showing no hesitation or shyness.

A social ritual evolves into a profession, a business. The women. lay down their terms, and the gomasthas have no choice but to accept, since the team is in great demand after their spectacular debut, and there is a paucity of options in the area. This portrait of a partnership of women well capable of managing their own professional affairs is developed in detail by the author. In the process what emerges clearly is the closeness between them. They are buddies, pals—terms which shake loose from the male-gendered moorings of common usage to apply perfectly to this female friendship. The image of these two friends making their quick, businesslike preparations and striding off to work side by side is, perhaps, unique in Indian literature and vividly captures the essence of this unusual relationship.

In addition to the ease and accord between them, the women are sensitive to each other's emotional states. When Bikhni returns from her visit to the Tohri prostitute quarter, she reports, 'I saw your son's wife there as well.' When Sanichari refuses to discuss the subject, she tactfully keeps quiet. But, as Bikhni intuits, despite her dismissive stance Sanichari is disturbed by the news, and broods about it. She thinks back, recalls details about the woman. And then suddenly, as the two sit companionably chewing tobacco after a meal, she says—

It was her fate. I wouldn't have turned her out after Budhua's death.

No, no, of course you wouldn't have.

Did she look very poor?

Very.

Sanichari fell silent.

This is the beginning of acceptance, a tentative groping towards finding extenuating reasons for Parbatia's defection, and compassion for her present situation. (In fact, compassion for the ageing prostitutes is uppermost in Bikhni's earlier account of their condition. There is no hint of disgust or moral aversion, just sympathy for women whose plight is possibly worse than their own.)

This delicate sensitivity to one another's inner emotional states shows itself again when Bikhni suddenly announces that she wants to go to Ranchi for a brief visit in the hope that she'll meet her son:

Sanichari said, Well, since you put it like that I won't say anything. You say you want to see your son. But will you come back soon? Or will you stay on there?

How can I? That day I had walked out of my home, and I met you by chance. If you hadn't been there that day, what would I have done?

. . . It was a three mile walk to the bus stop. Sanichari accompanied Bikhni, saw her onto the bus, advised her—It's eight rupees for a seat, squat in the aisle, you'll only have to pay two rupees.

Companionship, closeness, mutual dependency—these come through clearly, as does Sanichari's loneliness following Bikhni's departure:

At home, Sanichari felt restless. Out of habit she went into the forest to collect firewood, and returned with a bundle of dried twigs. Bikhni would never return emptyhanded. She'd bring back something or the other—either a couple of withered twigs or a length of rope she found on the path, or a pat of cowdung.

The news of Bikhni's death is handled by the author in her

characteristically understated style, which, through its un-emotional lack of emphasis, actually heightens impact. The passage immediately after Sanichari learns of Bikhni's death (p.88) is a good example of the way the author moves from negative—and weakening—emotions like fear, to self-knowledge and finally to positive action, without, however, minimizing the grief Sanichari feels. She will not cry for Bikhni: tears are a commodity now, part of a commercial transaction. Her loss lies deeper; but life must go on.

'This story is about survival,' the author insists. And the ending is a triumph of this major theme. After her discussion with Dulan, Sanichari's lingering inhibitions are removed. She is confident, in control, empowered. There is no inhibition in interacting with the prostitutes. She is relaxed and friendly, invites two ex-village girls, Parbatia and Gulbadan to join them—openly calling the former *bahu*—and emphasizes that this profession will stand them in good stead when, like her, they age, and other means of livelihood fail them. She offers to empower them as she herself has been empowered. And when confronting her social superiors she speaks up boldly, manipulating the situation cunningly to trap them in their own hypocrisy—if they restrain her they will expose their own greed. So they can only watch helplessly as she wails away their hopes of a profit on the side. She has learned her lessons well, and Dulan and Bikhni, both agents in the growth of her own agency, appear to have been internalized by her.

Nor is it just Sanichari who grows in stature. This triumph is not hers alone. Gulbadan, whose self-worth was shattered when her natural father Gambhir Singh ordered her to submit to the lust of his nephew, calling her a whore like her dead mother, is here in a spirit of vengeance. She turns lament into mockery as she casts a sneering wink at the nephew over her father's corpse. It is Sanichari, fully alive to the ironic overtones of this ritualized, commercialized system of lamentation, who foregrounds its subversive potential when she urges the prostitutes to use it as a means of revenge. By the end of this text, the custom of the rudali has been politicized. Not just a means of survival, it is an instrument of empowerment, a subaltern tool of revenge. The text literally closes on the clamouring, jubilant cries of the disempowered and the outcast, banded together to invert a howl of grief into a howl of triumph.

> 'I think being conscious about history is a primary condition of being a writer.'[1]

> 'As a writer I feel a commitment to my times, to mankind and to myself . . . for the last fourteen years I have written almost exclusively about the bonded labourers and the tribals, and about repression and protest, about their heroic endeavour for survival and their rights. I must have written a few hundred stories and 25 novels around these themes. . . .'[2]

> 'The background of 'Rudali' extends much beyond [the story]. I have travelled the whole of Palamou extensively by foot. I have seen all kinds of exploitation including bonded labour . . . A good number of my stories, including 'Bichan', 'Shikar', 'Jagmohan's Death', 'Shishu' and 'Rudali' are placed in this particular locale.'[3]

A major concern of the text is to establish itself as reality, not fiction. This is done in several ways. There are the various techniques of historicization already discussed, the refusal to individuate Sanichari—who could far too easily be positioned and perceived as the 'heroine' of the story—through physical or psychological description, to decontextualize her or put her centre-stage out of proportion to her role as part of a community. There is the materiality of the text, its relentless desentimentalization, the reiterated message that considerations of the stomach are primary, beyond censure, outweighing emotion or socio-religious convention, and the driving force behind all action. No romantic clichés are permitted to stand, nor idealized notions of village life. Material details of food production, labour, the struggle to survive, are stressed by the author. The harsh realities of poverty, exploitation and death are exposed in brutal detail with all their attendant degradation. (For example, when

---

1. Interview with Mahasweta Devi on 26.5.93.
2. Statement by Mahasweta Devi at the Frankfurt Book Fair, 1986, as part of the Indian Presentation. Unpublished essay.
3. Interview with Mahasweta Devi on 26.5.93. The stories mentioned are available in English translation as part of her *Selected Works* (Seagull, Calcutta, forthcoming).

Sanichari's brother- and sister-in-law die, everyone explains the fact that she and her husband don't shed any tears by the sentiment that their grief must have hardened into stone within them, at the frequent deaths in the family. Sanichari, however, is relieved. Two less mouths to feed on the meagre scrapings they bring home: At least the survivors' stomachs will be full.)

Even the characters in the story are not intended to be fictional. They—or their prototypes—exist outside the story.

> Sanichari is also from this locality . . . And this [sense of a community] is very important. It is so important to me now, that I have started to write followups of these stories . . . For example you have Dulan ganju. His son gets killed. I have written a report in *Aajkal.* I am yet to write the last story. Then this Dulan episode will be complete. Dhatua's son is killed by the landlord. He gets married and the landlord wants to have his wife on the first night. This story is based on a real incident. He was burnt to death. When I went to USA they asked me about this incident, which they read about in *New York Times.* The news was first published in *Times Of India* . . . In my story Dulan receives books from someone. But since he cannot read he keeps the books aside. His grandson asks him, 'What are you keeping there?' The grandson and his wife have learnt reading and writing. Now this grandson gets killed. The wife is rescued. Dulan goes back to his books. Towards the end of the story Dulan takes the books with him and joins the adult literacy class. Now he has to learn the alphabet. He wants to read what is written there. The story ends here. So the Dulan you have seen in 'Rudali' or in 'Bichan', has become contemporary. He reaches the present, 1993. I want to bring them up to 1993 . . .[1]

Real details of real poverty, learnt at firsthand. Real characters with real life histories. And a text which is not constructed as a linear narrative. The narrative makes no attempt to move aggressively or concentratedly to a denouement: this is to be read as reality, not fiction; not even

---

1. Interview with Mahasweta Devi on 26.5.93.

a 'fictionalizing' of the real. The 'storyline' is scarcely privileged over the space given to segments of oral history or social
critique. There is no concern with building character, atmosphere or suspense. The narrative begins informally, slips
into a life at some indistinct point. There is no dramatic
opening incident, no frozen moment lending purpose and
justification to the starting point: there is, in other words, no
acknowledgement of a fictionalization. The opening paragraph itself casually spans years of Sanichari's life. The same
freedom from temporal linearity continues to mark the narrative. The narrating voice moves back in time in an
informal, arbitrary manner, stopping to comment and to add
contextual details which continuously anchor the private story
in the more public history. This loosely looped narrative
approach closely approximates the oral form of reminiscence
and conversation, the 'primary source' of journalistic reporting and oral history. As in life, there is space for digression,
comment.

And yet, the anti-fictiveness of the work must itself be
seen as a deliberate construct, part of an agenda, deliberately
aimed at creating the effect of 'realism'. The author uses the
movement of Sanichari's evolution to empowerment as the
organizing principle around which other aspects of the
agenda, such as the critique of the socio-economic system, are
arranged. She uses the composite character of Dulan ganju to
embody the politicized subaltern. She skilfully breaks narration with dialogue, 'showing' rather than 'telling'—
allowing the characters to speak for themselves and simultaneously establishing authenticity. She punctuates this
discourse of deprivation with death, orchestrating it so that
each death grows progressively closer and more devastating to
the central character, maintaining as ironic counterpoint
those other deaths, the deaths of the rich. Her masterful use of
irony is perhaps her most powerful creative tool. In her hands
the social custom of rudalis accumulates rich layers of ironic
symbolism, variously explicated by Dulan and Sanichari, until
it takes on all the power of a weapon of subversion. In fact, the
entire text is infused with ironic comment, not least from her
own stance of 'no comment' while narrating the most
outrageously hypocritical events. The savage wit of her ironic
tone is as powerful an indictment as the one she so carefully
builds up through her text—achieved not with the crusading

righteous indignation of the outraged outsider but, much more tellingly, with the cutting cynicism of the insider to whom none of this, alas, is new.

As Mahasweta Devi herself claims, her work as a journalist, creative writer and activist overlap: 'As a journalist I play the same role as an editor. I travel extensively in the villages and collect information about people's sufferings, complaints, political exploitation, their protests and write about these in the press . . . As an editor, journalist and writer I experience no conflict between the three roles.'[1] Gayatri Chakravorty Spivak feels that Mahasweta Devi's 'writing and her activism reflect one another, that they are precisely that— "a folding back upon" one another—reflection in the root sense . . . Indeed, if one reads carefully, one may be seen as the other's *differance*.'[2] I see 'Rudali', rather, as part of, integrated with, the activism—as activist fiction. It sets out to support the process of struggle she writes about—by enlightening, educating, celebrating, reaffirming and inspiring. It participates in the struggle by attacking, through accusation and exposure, the exploitative system the struggle targets and the individuals through whom this system functions. Fiction is honed into a weapon by being presented as its apparent opposite, reportage. Just as Dulan's work in 'Rudali' is consciousness-raising, 'Rudali's' work is conscientizing. 'This relationship: a witnessing love and a supplementing collective struggle, is the relationship between [Mahasweta Devi's] "literary" writing and her activism' says Spivak, elaborating on her earlier comment.[3] True, Ms Spivak speaks of a later collection of fictive works; but it is hard to differentiate thus between the 'literary' writing and the activism. The creative writing is as much part of her deeply engaged, politicized and committed consciousness as is any other form of activism, and it works towards the same goal. 'Rudali', for example, is more than journalism, more than fiction, and wholly political.

---

1. Statement by Mahasweta Devi at the Frankfurt Book Fair, 1986.
2. Gayatri Chakravorty Spivak, *Imaginary Maps* (Thema, Calcutta, 1984), Translator's Preface.
3. Gayatri Chakravorty Spivak, *Imaginary Maps* (Thema, Calcutta, 1984), Appendix.

II

Mahasweta Devi may see her text as part of the discourse of class rather than gender, but to Usha Ganguli 'Rudali' is powerful precisely because it is a woman's story:

> I wanted to write about Indian women, about their problems, their sufferings, social prejudices etc. I produced *Bama* at that time, which contained three different stories of three different women, but there were no Indian women in it. 'What about her story, her struggle?' This question was haunting me all the time . . . Suddenly 'Rudali', which I had read long ago, came to mind, and I started writing down a few things. Initially I wrote two scenes: in one Sanichari wears the earrings, and the other was Parbatia's confrontation with Sanichari. Incidentally, neither of the scenes are in the original story. I couldn't stop thinking of 'Rudali' . . . There are two subjects that I have wanted to work with. One is how the political parties are exploiting our religion . . . The other is the women's problem. I haven't found any suitable Indian play dealing with these problems . . . If a man had directed *Rudali* I know it would have been totally different. For example, the relationship between Sanichari and Bikhni was based solely on my inner experiences. I also wanted to show different kinds and shades of women in *Rudali*.[1]

By interpreting it as a woman's story, she strips the original text of its class specificity, and in the process dehistoricizes it, not entirely, perhaps, but certainly to a significant extent:

> [Sanichari and Bikhni] don't appeal to me simply because they belong to a different class. There is something very human in them, and that breaks the class barrier. Everybody is able to communicate with them, their struggle becomes everybody's struggle . . . I strongly believe that *Rudali* is a women's text. I believe that the Indian woman, whether it's Sanichari or someone from the middle or upper class, is highly exploited in our society. Somehow in *Rudali* I see Sanichari protesting against society on the whole. Somebody told

---

1. Interview with Usha Ganguli on 20.4.93

me that *Rudali* is a play about a village. I don't agree. It
is not about a particular village or a city or even about a
particular character, but about all of us: Sanichari
represents women in general. It is the humanistic
element that makes it acceptable to all of us . . .[1]

The easy term 'all of us' with its humanist, universalizing,
all-embracing connotations in fact disguises an opposite
significance. It signifies something closer to 'those like us'.
In other words it is exclusive rather than inclusive, and
presupposes a consonance of values, tastes, and ideas which in
turn presupposes specifics of class and social background.

    This leads us straight to my next point, which concerns
aims—what is the purpose of each of these texts? At whom are
they aimed? The Mahasweta Devi story grows out of her own
firsthand knowledge of the specific socio-economic and
historic situation she is writing about. Hers is not an urban
'idea' of rural reality, derived at one remove from other
media, although the ideological filter which mediates the
choice and viewpoint of what she depicts determines an
agenda which shapes the text.

    There is, in her work, an awareness of an urban literate
audience insofar as she takes care to explode comfortable
myths about village life. But this awareness does not lead to
any compromise in presentation (as her rejection of narrative
convention indicates), nor any attempt at 'translating' for the
benefit of those unfamiliar with the milieu she depicts.
When Mahasweta Devi was questioned about the harsh, often
shocking content—to urban middle-class sensibilities—of
many of her stories, she firmly rejected the idea that she
wrote to shock, or, as she put it, used her writing as a 'stunt'.
Urban society was ignorant about rural life, and therefore
perceived the grim facts as sensationalism. 'In Kalahandi
they are selling their children. You have not seen it, but it is
real. I cannot help it, it happens to be a fact that my
readership is middle class. If they do not know about these
things what can I do about it?'[2] Experience and factual detail is
the ground on which her fiction is inscribed. The opposite
process pertains in the case of the play. The starting impulse

---

1. Interview with Usha Ganguli on 20.4.93
2. Interview with Mahasweta Devi on 26.5.93.

there is to produce good theatre for an urban audience, theatre which will address concerns common to 'all of us'. A text is chosen which offers material for such theatre. Studies are undertaken to research the factual detail necessary to create an 'authentic' atmosphere. These are adapted or rejected according to the requirements of that theatre and that audience. Thus the play, both in its construct of the 'real' and its attempts to make that 'reality' more accessible to those unfamiliar with it, is wholly urban.

Also, Usha Ganguli's commitment to socio-realistic proscenium theatre, with its imperatives of a linear storyline and definite structure, causes her to interpret the original text to fit in with the demands and restrictions of this performance form, resulting in significant structural changes.

These basic realignments of perspective govern the adaptation, as this section of the paper will establish through a detailed study of the similarities and differences between the two texts, story and play. Undoubtedly a creative adaptation need not faithfully echo the original, and if the director had claimed only a basic inspiration from the original, a kind of 'loosely based on' status, the terms of this analysis would have been very different. However, the opposite is true. The director has striven to be faithful to the original, down to inviting the author to participate in the adaptation/scriptwriting process; and the author, self-confessedly wary about her work being turned into plays and films, has approved of the production, affirming in public that the director has retained the spirit of the original: 'Whenever someone adapts my story into a play or a film I always fear that the stress will be shifted. The play has retained the stress as it is in my story. . . not deviated from it.'[1]

In this context, changes and their meaning accrue a special significance. Many of these are microlevel shifts and alterations which cohere to form a web of signification, reflecting fundamental ideological positions. This section will, therefore, examine the nature of these alterations in structure and content scene by scene, analysing the reasons behind them and how the text begins to signify differently as a result.

The prose text, as already discussed, introduces a socio-

---

1. Interview with Mahasweta Devi on 26.5.93.

economic situation simultaneously with the central character, thereby contextualizing her story from the start. It slips into the tale at some undifferentiated point in time. The play, likewise, establishes the situation of Sanichari's life in an 'undramatic' manner: a day in the life of . . .

Before the stage lightens we hear the chakki—an aural-cum-visual metaphor (grinding poverty, labour, food) for Sanichari's existence. The set design carefully suggests 'real' poverty with a few well placed props. On stage are Sanichari (grinding wheat), her dying son Budhua on a charpoy, her physically feeble but sharp-tongued old mother-in-law Somri wrapped in a quilt, and her little grandson Haroa lying under the charpoy playing with a toy. We learn right off that Sanichari is desperately poor, and the only provider in that household.With the first scene we are plunged into inter-personal family tensions, unlike in the story where the tension between classes is emphasized rather than those within families. The friction between her mother-in-law and her, mentioned by the way in the story, is used here to underscore Sanichari's lonely, hard existence, unappreciated and cursed as manhoos by the old woman, who blames her for all the misfortunes of their lives. Sanichari snaps back at her with the retort left unspoken in the story: that being born on a Saturday hasn't brought her any worse luck than it has those born on 'luckier' days.

Here she has been constructed very much as the strong matriarch, able to answer back, the provider and decision-maker in her home. Significantly, the relationship between Sanichari and her son has been altered: he is weak and ineffectual rather than gentle and supportive. He seeks *her* advice on whether or not his wife should be allowed to work for Lachman Singh. In the story, as we have seen, he deals with the same issue independently and resourcefully. Here he even asks 'Why not?'when she refuses. And *she* tells *him* the fate of young women who work for the malik-mahajan. A few seconds later a neighbouring child is sent to beg a few sticks to light their stove with. Sanichari's response is a refusal, because the child's mother has not paid for something she had ground for her the previous week. Only after Budhua intercedes does she grudgingly give in. Seconds later the child grabs at Haroa's toy. He complains and she is chased out. This kind of petty friction amongst villagers is completely absent from Mahasweta Devi's story. All we see there is cooperation and generosity amongst them. Soon Parbatia returns. The open hostility between Sanichari and her is in direct contradiction to the story, which states that despite her resentment Sanichari found herself unable to reprimand her daughter-in-law. There Parbatia is not directly shown, just discussed as having an 'appetite' for more than their spartan household could supply. Here she *is* shown—as aggressive, hostile, sly, greedy and extremely selfish. She spends the precious rupees needed for medicine on ornaments for herself (in the story it's food), refuses to help out with household chores, flays her husband for being less than virile and therefore less than a man, and taunts him and Sanichari by comparing him unfavourably to Lachman Singh— 'He may be a devil, but at least he's a man! Not like this one, coughing his lungs out all day!'[1] Sanichari moves to strike her, and they grapple. They break apart at the entry of Lachmi, who is positioned as a caring, supportive neighbour, always ready with soothing advice or a helping hand, invariably counter-balancing a more malicious woman character in any given scene (here Somri, Parbatia).

Throughout, Budhua has been a helpless spectator, once pleading weakly, 'Let it be, ma,' to which neither woman pays any attention. He doesn't defend himself, it's his mother who springs to his defence. The cruel jibes Parbatia makes, and her privileging 'macho' manhood over any kind of class or family loyalty are alien to Mahasweta Devi's story, as is the physical violence between women or members of the same class.

Except for the weak and helpless man and boy, the entire first scene is played between women: two strong women, Sanichari (responsible, stoic, someone who bears up and comes through) and her opposite, Parbatia (driven, self-absorbed, self-indulgent), bracketed by two 'supporting' char-acters, one negative (Somri: critical, demanding, but helpless) and the other, her opposite, supportive (Lachmi: gentle, sympathetic, positive). This cleanly balanced symmetry with its clearcut value alignments is fairly typical of the rest of the play. A negative presence is balanced by a positive one.

---

1. Usha Ganguli, *Rudali,* a play in Hindi. This and all subsequent quotations from the play are tfrom my translation in this volume.

According to the director, it is more 'realistic' to show petty carping and a lack of generosity amongst members of the village community than to present the unproblematized harmony that Mahasweta Devi shows. To 'balance out the picture', therefore, the play takes care to present both black and white.

If the first scene had introduced us to Parbatia's callous selfishness, the second, in which Budhua dies, blackens her beyond redemption. We see her titivating while her husband coughs desperately, almost choking. She continues, indifferent. She 'slaps away her child's hand when he, innocently wondering, fingers her things. Reluctantly, upon being repeatedly urged by Somri, she bestirs herself to hand Budhua some water, addressing him offensively and rudely. He is too weak to hold the container and drops it. Startled, but hiding the situation from the questioning old woman, she darts off-stage to gather her things. She has obviously made up her mind to leave since she can see her husband is about to die. Sanichari enters, so she hides her intention and belongings. When Sanichari pleads with her to fetch the vaid (traditional doctor) she refuses point blank. Finally Sanichari asks her to watch over Budhua and herself goes to fetch the vaid. At once Parbatia picks up her bundle, and, pausing once near her son, runs off. Later in the scene we are informed that she has run off with whatever money there was in the house. In Mahasweta Devi's story the handling of the Parbatia issue is very different. She is described as a dain but at the same time we are shown Budhua's sensitive understanding of the hungers that drive her. She is not painted as black as she is here, and at the end, after *she* makes the first overture, is invited back into the fold by Sanichari. In the play, she spurns the invitation, remaining to the last as hostile—and as marginalized—as in the beginning.

When questioned about the change in the treatment of Parbatia, Usha Ganguli insisted that she had followed the text: 'When I visualize a character I don't put any value judgement. When I spoke to Mahasweta Devi, she requested me not to portray Parbatia as someone bad, but as someone who was merely trying to survive. . . [My treatment of Parbatia] is all in the story.'[1] And yet this is clearly not true.

---

1. Interview with Usha Ganguli on 20.4.93

Even if one allows for interpretive leeway, there are the damning extras, like stealing the meagre household funds, which makes her a thief as well. What could have motivated this blackwashing exercise? One explanation could be architectural: the urge to construct a strong anti-Sanichari character/relationship to balance the strong Sanichari-Bikhni alignment that marks the rest of the play. As we have seen, this tendency towards a balancing of poles is very characteristic of the play, and is probably determined by the demand for a strong, balanced script suited to this particular genre of theatre. (Even the latter part of the same scene shows us, by way of the larger community, two women gossiping maliciously and two being protective of Sanichari as they discuss the scandal of Parbatia's absence.)

In its treatment of the way the community rallies around, offers whatever little it can, takes over chores and helps out, the play is in consonance with the story, except, as mentioned earlier, when the director feels it necessary to balance kindness with a little malice for the sake of 'realism.' When Sanichari returns with the vaid, we see for the first time a member of a higher class/caste. Like his counterpart in the story, this vaid is contemptuous and condescending, callous and mercenary. His total insensitivity to her grief and insistence on being paid on the spot, followed by the arrival of her co-villagers led by Dulan, to pitch in and help, followed by the discovery that Parbatia has absconded with the family funds, leave Sanichari no time for private mourning. This is the first family death we are shown, and the play, like the story, establishes how the private space of grief is invaded and taken over by socio-economic circumstances. In order to raise the cash for the obligatory religious ritual expenses she has to sell her chåkki, at Dulan's suggestion, although this is her only means of livelihood. As Bijua, a co-villager says, 'Living is tough for us poor people, but dying is even worse.'

Dulan, as in the story, is a source of support, but nowhere near the canny strategy-spinner that he is in the original. There are telling slips: Dulan asks Bijua, 'Now tell me, what else will we need?' Considering that these are timeworn customs, that little bit of dialogic emphasis can only be for the benefit of an urban audience. Surely Dulan does not need to have such things explained to him!

In scene three we meet a young Haroa. This is the only

other male family member we see, and he is as weak as his
father. He sounds like a petulant, sulky boy and is shown as
preoccupied with his appearance, combing his hair, etc.—
signs we have come to identify with Parbatia's fecklessness.
He airs his grievances over the job his grandmother has
managed to arrange with great difficulty, at Lachman
Singh's: he is paid a pittance, is overworked, gets beaten by
his master's son, is abused, and so on. Sanichari's response to
his complaints is to advocate acquiescence ('That's a poor
man's fate, beta—the kicks of his master.') and subservience.
It is hard to imagine any of the villagers in Mahasweta
Devi's story offering similar advice to one of their own.

Community relations are slanted differently from the
story: when Bijua enters we see a conversation between
equals, informal and relaxed. He brings news of some work
in Lachman's house—but he also brings news of Parbatia: she
is a whore in Tohri, has aged beyond her years. His purpose
in telling her this is gossip. In the story, Sanichari's fellow
villagers keep it from her out of concern for her feelings.
Dulan brings it up at the end only to reassure her. Bikhni
brings her news of Parbatia in quite a different spirit—as
something intimate shared between two close friends,
something she knows matters—rather than, as here, in a
gossipy vein.

The first time we see a community of women together is
in scene four. It begins with a group of village women—and
Misri accuses Sanichari of shortchanging her. There is a
bitter quarrel. Lachmi the peacekeeper intervenes: balance
again. Community interaction continues: Natua brings
Sanichari the tally of vegetables sold that day—he is helping
her out, as in the original, by peddling her vegetables in the
marketplace, but, unlike the original, is also fiddling the
accounts: a quid pro quo only the rich would be capable of in
Mahasweta Devi's story.

The quarrel with Haroa, which follows, is treated
differently from the story. What does this sequence signify?
He lies about attending work till Sanichari confronts him
with witnesses. She gives him an ultimatum—he defiantly
says he'll leave. Then he turns on her the same accusation his
mother did, almost an echo: 'Can't provide a square meal,
and orders me around!' He accuses her of keeping his great
grandmother and mother hungry and killing his father.

'She's a dain, she's finished off all the others, now she'll devour me.' Inflamed, Sanichari attacks him. Dulan and Lachmi hold her back. The boy walks out, reiterating the terrible accusations, all the more treacherous because they come from someone she has loved and raised. He ends by cursing her—'You'll have to stay here all alone'—a curse that will come terribly true.

This is the only other family relationship with a male that we are shown in the play, and it ends in betrayal. After years of caring and nurture, the boy, when provoked, so easily turns against his grandmother and joins in the chorus of defamation: family bonds are shown as fragile, family relationships as self-serving. The sequence further underscores Sanichari's solitude and isolation, betrayed by those who should, by virtue of blood and upbringing, be closest to her. In the story Haroa is never shown as attacking his grandmother. He starts working conscientiously enough, then gradually loses interest, begins to spend his money on little indulgences and hang around with the fairground folk, till one day, soon after being thrashed and threatened by her, he runs away. His restlessness drives him to search for a different life, but there is no cruelty or vindictiveness towards the grandmother. The effect of the changed scenario in the play is, of course, to create more sympathy for lonely, unappreciated, hardworking Sanichari and to reaffirm that the male sex is selfish and unreliable. In the story, exploitation forms part of the discourse of class. In the play, it is gendered.

As scene five opens, we see Bikhni against a fairground setting, and for the first time the mood of the play lightens. She is a feisty, spirited personality, colourful and blunt of speech, with an irrepressible impudence. The two women literally bump into each other, as in the story. As they bring each other up to date, Bikhni asks with concern if Sanichari has eaten that day—she looks famished. Bikhni insists on sharing her snack with her. This is the first time in the play that anyone at all expresses a personal concern for Sanichari, noticing her enough to notice that she looks hungry. She's always been taken for granted. The first touch of concern and caring comes, not from one of her family, but from this outsider who will soon grow closer than any blood relation. Bikhni too has been betrayed and abandoned by her son. Both women have lost their sources of support in their old age. Unlike in the story, where the supportive Sanichari-Budhua mother-son relationship is balanced against Bikhni's son's treachery, here there are no redeeming comparisons or contrasts. Males are treacherous, regardless of family ties.

Scene six is structurally the core of the play. The purpose of the scene is to establish the bonding between the two women. In that sense, it is at the heart of the play. In the story, this closeness between the women is allowed to emerge through the text in a less spotlit manner. It is revealed through the way they cohere as a team, work together, share their problems and good times. In the play the necessity for a tight dramatic structure makes it important to halt the grim logic of this sad narrative with a scene which highlights the warm tenderness between the women; a visual foregrounding which heightens the sense of loss and loneliness at the end of the play.

The scene begins with Bikhni combing and grooming Sanichari's hair—an intimate, woman-to-woman activity which signifies caring and tenderness. They affectionately recall each other as little girls playing together—probably the last time in both their lives that they felt free. Sanichari says, 'Where did I ever get the time to do my hair or dress up, Bikhni? My life has been nothing but the stove, the chakki, and outside jobs.' Bikhni replies, 'Such is a woman's lot.' Sanichari repeats, 'My whole life has been spent working, working.' Sympathetically, Bikhni echoes, 'What a life! Full of tears, sorrow,' but Sanichari contradicts her. 'No, I never had the time to weep.' She mentions that they call her dain— and Bikhni explodes in anger. 'Which son of a bitch dares call you a dain? I'll scratch his eyes out! Don't worry, Sanichari, you'll see, everything will turn out fine. I'll get hold of some fertilizer from the government office and start growing vegetables once again, and I'll sell them myself in the market.' She offers a loyalty and support Sanichari's own kith and kin have refused her. When Sanichari expresses her gratitude for all the hard work Bikhni has done around the house, Bikhni answers, 'Why are you keeping a tally?' She already feels this is her home.

In the story, by detailing another close loving relationship between Sanichari and Budhua, the author balances the two relationships, showing simultaneously that closeness between male and female family members is possible. In the play, this friendship is the only close, caring relationship Sanichari is shown as experiencing; and the focus of the play naturally tightens onto the bonding between these two women.

On impulse, Bikhni fetches a pair of earrings and puts them on Sanichari. 'I had bought them at the mela for myself. Just see how nice they look!' she says. Sanichari protests, shy and awkward. Bikhni shushes her and fetches a mirror. 'Go ahead, take a good look.' Sanichari is moved. 'This is the first time in my whole life that anyone has given me a gift . . . no, no, once my husband also . . .'

As the scene continues Sanichari talks of how she was coerced into paying twice over for the kriya ceremony after her husband's death, and incurred a debt in order to do so. Bikhni asks, 'D'you mean to say that the brahmins of Tohri village are different from the brahmins of Tahad village?' and Sanichari replies, 'Who knows . . . the thakurs and brahmins are all in this together. They control everything. It took me five years to pay off my debt to the thakur.' The play thus verbalizes the questions raised by implication in the story, which sarcastically narrates the events in a dry, matter-of-fact tone, leaving the questions and judgements in the mind of the reader. This shift in presentation makes it more explicit (by raising the questions the play ensures that the audience considers them too), but also positions the whole issue as one of personal attitudes, Sanichari's and Bikhni's. In the story, no one character is voicing the cynicism. The dry narration causes the hypocrisy and exploitation to be seen as inherent to the larger condition. By working Sanichari's past into an intimate conversation between friends, the play text personalizes it. It becomes more private, the singular tale of a single human being, whereas as part of the general narration of the story it was part of a larger discourse, more clearly located in the stream of local history.

This central scene establishes the warm affection between the two women with a poignant sensitivity. After thanking her for all that she has done, Sanichari says, 'I'm telling you, Bikhni, in my whole life nobody has ever done so much for me. No one has even thought of me as a human being!' As they lie down side by side, preparing to sleep, she says, 'You know, when I was a girl my mother used to always

tell me that a woman's worst enemy was other women . . .
And Bikhni scoffs, 'Arre, that's all stuff made up by men.
This succinct exchange encapsulates a whole cultural history of
socialization and psychological indoctrination of women by a
patriarchal social system which seeks to foster distrust between
them, reinforced by the internalization of such myths and
stereotypes by the women themselves. Bikhni's comment is in
fact a highly sophisticated response in feminist terms,
identifying and dismissing the source of such divisive
thinking. Sisterhood and solidarity are graphically
established in this one scene.

The next scene returns us to grim reality. Sanichari and
Bikhni count their coins—they are down to their last few
rupees, and the vegetable patch is bare. How are they to
survive? However, this time Sanichari is not shouldering the
burden alone. Bikhni reiterates her commitment to the
relationship: 'What's this "your" money business? . . . You
still haven't accepted me as your own, Sanichari.' They are
interrrupted by Misri (the malicious neighbour) who
badmouths them as usual, immediately balanced by Lachmi
(the friendly neighbour) with whom they share a lighter
moment. Dulan enters, and they ask him for advice. Here
again there are little, telling changes in characterization.
Instead of Dulan telling the women that the poor have to carve
out their own ways of earning, as he does in the story, the
dialogue is exactly reversed, and it is Bikhni who imparts
this bit of philosophical wisdom to her male co-villager.
Dulan then tells them to seek jobs as construction workers; but
Lachmi protests. Surely they are too old now for that kind of
hard labour? At this point Dulan comes up with his
iconoclastic suggestion of picking up a black stone and
collecting money in the marketplace by claiming it was found
as the result of a dream vision. Bikhni applauds this
suggestion immediately, more vigorously than in the
original; but Sanichari is outraged, far more emphatically so
than in the story. The same Sanichari who in the previous
scene was being cynical about the gods of the poor now
exclaims, 'Quiet! Making mockery of the gods! All my life
I've worked hard to earn my living—and now, in my old age,
am I to fool around like this with something sacred?!' Her
response in the story is in a lighter vein, more cognisant of
the irreverent humour in Dulan's tongue-in-cheek suggestion.

Here, as in the story, Dulan explicates his philosophy that sin is a mental attitude. With the same example of the old woman and the holy oil which he gives in the original text, he concludes that one's stomach comes before the gods. For the sake of the stomach one can do anything. At this point Bijua bursts in with the news of Bhairav Singh's murder. All the complex socio-economic analysis and strongly constructed critique associated with this sequence in the original is simplified into Bijua's 'The world of the wealthy is different from ours. For the sake of money, a mother can kill her son, a son his mother' and his incredulous reply, when Dulan (once more cast as much more credulous—un'real'istically so?—than in the original) asks if the murderer has been arrested: 'Are you crazy? Will the police arrest someone like him? These people have the power of money—the law, the police, the government, are all firmly in their grasp.' In Mahasweta Devi's text, no villager would have asked such a foolish question. Here, so the audience can hear this reply, has 'realism' been sacrificed to a good line? Next, Dulan suggests to Sanichari and Bikhni that they offer themselves as rudalis. Bikhni asks, 'Are there no family members to weep for him?' and Dulan counters with, 'Only the families of the poor mourn their dead. The rich households have to hire mourners.'

It is precisely because so much of the dialogue echoes the original text, whole lines and sequences translated literally from it, that the shifts and changes take on a special significance. The exchange between Sanichari and Dulan which follows, for example, is close to the original: She protests her inability to cry, referring to the incident when she sat under a tree, determined to cry for her husband, but couldn't make a single tear materialize. (What is totally elided over in this passing reference is the material context of bonded labour and Dulan's positive intervention which gave direction to her confused resentment.) Dulan gives her his 'this crying is work' speech. Then Lachmi inserts a question that no fellow villager articulates in the original—'Couldn't you think of some other work for them than sitting and mourning alongside cheap whores!' In the story, the social acceptability of the profession of rudalis is not even a concern at the village level. It is, in fact, the opposite concern—not the question of her doing work fit for prostitutes but of inviting

them to work with *her* that worries Sanichari; and she asks
Dulan if the village will turn against her for it. Here, Dulan's
response to Lachmi—'A job's a job'—is said in much the same
manner as he quietens Sanichari's misgivings in the
original. Bikhni, who is much more positive, adaptable and
venturesome, as in the original, settles the matter by giving
the idea her wholehearted approval. And then Dulan does
something so far from the spirit of the original that it raises
important questions regarding the differing perceptions of
intra-community, intra-class relationships in the story and
the play: he asks them for a commission. Sanichari says, 'You
so-and-so, you want a cut, do you!' And he retorts, 'So what's
wrong with that? Everyone from the Prime Minister down to
the lowest untouchable takes cuts.' Whereupon Bikhni uses a
phrase to describe him which, in the original, is used with
grudging respect by an outwitted member of a higher class, 'A
hundred bastards must have died to give birth to a rascal like
you.'

As one proceeds through the play, there is a growing
realization that relations within the community are shown as
far less supportive, generous and harmonious than in the
original. At no time in Mahasweta Devi's text does one come
across members of the same class exploiting one another,
leave alone justifying the exploitation as part of the system, as
the way things are done. Dulan provides Sanichari with work
more than once, even negotiates on her behalf, but the
question of making money off a fellow villager in distress
does not arise. No doubt the play views its own position as a
more 'realistic' one, and Mahasweta Devi's very different
portrayal of community as 'idealistic.' The polarity of these
two terms has come up in the director's language when
discussing certain changes in the play (more of that later).
Another concern of the play is to gender the discourse of
exploitation: the women have been consistently shown as
exploited, emotionally and financially, by the men. This
action of Dulan's further establishes this position.

Scene eight shows us Sanichari and Bikhni becoming
rudalis. It begins with the post-death rites, punctuated with
acidic comments and ribald laughter from the three lively
prostitutes who have been hired as rudalis. Totally
irrepressible, they undermine the solemn hypocrisy of the
occasion, where the murderer plays the grief-stricken son and

rich relatives with gun-toting bodyguards stride in to pay their last respects. As in the story, the blatant conflation of prestige and social status with the lavishness of the funerary rites is shown, and this includes rudalis. But the women are subversive—colourful of language and appearance, cheeky, loud and quite capable of holding their own in the face of snubs and disapproval. When they are chided for unseemliness and ingratitude, they retort sharply, 'Yes, yes, the master was like a god to us! He made whores of us, fed and clothed us and on his death left us five whole rupees!' In the play it is only the prostitutes who are shown boldly talking back to social superiors and using sly humour to puncture their self-esteem. The social disapproval in which they exist has given them liberties denied those within the perimeter of social acceptability. They are beyond censure, and in a society which represses through the mechanism of censure, this means freedom. In fact, their gaiety and uninhibited manner creates a very different image of them from that of the story, in which they are consistently talked of and portrayed as suffering and labour-driven like the poor village women.

When Dulan enters with Sanichari and Bikhni, he bargains on their behalf, as in the original, using his insider knowledge of budgets as leverage. But there is a line he speaks in the process which is completely alien to his value system as constructed in the story: 'Only five rupees! For women from decent homes!' By implication he is drawing a derogatory distinction between 'decent' and 'indecent' women, which reflects Lachmi's concern about the acceptability of working alongside prostitutes: a distinction never made in the story. Tiny touches, but telling.

The scene closes on the melodramatic wailing and lamentation raised by Sanichari and Bikhni. The effect of the chorused cries is gripping. There is no space for subversion, humour or irony here. In the story, the business of rudalis is treated with tongue firmly in cheek. We are told how 'effective' Sanichari and Bikhni are, but always from a cynical perspective: their own, Dulan's or the author's. Seeing them mourn and hearing the detailed laments they chant combines to generate a moment of powerful theatre, but the ironic symbolism with which Mahasweta Devi infuses the act is missing here.

In scene nine we see Sanichari and Bikhni as seasoned

rudalis, settled into a routine. They gossip about their social superiors' miserly ways—one recalls the sharply critical views expressed by Sanichari and her peers in the original story. But there is a telling difference. Here they mock the merchant-traders (one step lower on the socio-economic/caste rung than the landholder-masters) for their attempt to emulate the thakurs. In other words, they draw a distinction between the two upper classes, favouring one over the other. This is never done in the original. The upper castes are 'other', regardless of hierarchies amongst them. After the good neighbour/bad neighbour routine which seems to be the pattern of community relations in the play, Nathuni Singh's middle wife arrives to see Sanichari. It is a secret visit, a departure from the norm for a thakurain to be visiting this lowcaste home. (In the original, she sends for Sanichari.) In the sequence that follows we see, for the first time, a member of the dominant class, albeit of the same sex: an upper class/caste mistress with her 'serfs.' She enters. They have hurriedly prepared a seat for her. She sits. They wash, dry and touch her feet. There is no ironic tone to any of this. It is projected and played as normative social etiquette. Sanichari asks why she has taken the trouble of visiting them when she could have sent for them instead. The thakurain ignores the question and abruptly announces, 'You'll have to take the early morning bus to Lohri village tomorrow.' The conversation that follows is an interesting amalgam of portions lifted in context from the original and lines put together from other characters and sequences. Echoing the story, Bikhni asks, when the thakurain says her father is dying of smallpox, 'But I thought only the poor got that disease?' Obviously disease is no respecter of social barriers, and it's class-bound nature is a myth. The thakurain, who has internalized the patriarchal values of her class (she boasts of how feared and powerful her father was, how villagers quaked at the sight of him, of how she plans to turn her in-laws green with envy at the lavish splendour of his funerary ceremonies), suffers the discrimination of those same values being turned against her for being the mother of a mere girl, for having contributed no heirs to the family. Full of spite, she washes family dirty linen for Sanichari and Bikhni, giving them shocking details of family cruelty which, in the original story, formed part of Dulan's scathing subaltern perspective. Here it is she

who accuses her in-laws of criminal neglect: 'All day long his old mother would lie rotting in her own piss and shit, while her son counted the days till the old woman popped off and he could lay his hands on all her wealth!' It is she who points out the hypocrisy of allowing her upper-caste mother-in-law to be tended by untouchables—what about loss of caste? An interesting shift takes place when these lines are spoken by the thakurain instead of Dulan. After all, an indictment turned on her own class and community, especially when she still wholly identifies with them, has a totally different impact than a harsh critique from below. Self-criticism is almost a virtue. Moreover, motives of malice and spite have a reductive effect when they replace a critique of a class and its values which is posited as justified. Also—this secretive visit by one woman to two others, in which she talks of personal matters and reveals her own hurt at being discriminated against, signifies a cross-class gender bonding which is, in fact, illusory. The visual impression created by the scene, the secrecy, the intimacy emphasized by the darkness, the three women in close conversation, signals a closeness which is denied by the facts, which are that the thakurain is there for her own purpose: she wishes to hire their services as rudalis. There are no connections beyond the mistress-servant relationship.

In scene ten Sanichari is alone again, returned to solitude without her companion. Dulan enters, and, instead of reassurance or emotional support, offers the prediction that Bikhni will not return. After all, he says, why should she leave her son and grandchild, a home where she'll be pampered and loved, to come back here and earn her own living? One cannot help comparing this insensitivity to the delicacy with which the community bolsters Sanichari's morale in the original story. Sanichari asserts that having given her word, Bikhni will surely return. After all, she has her profession to consider.

The theme of Dulan the exploiter making a commission off their labour continues. He tells her that thakur Gambhir Singh is dying. He has stipulated that one lakh of rupees is to be spent on his death ceremonies. Sanichari must not let this opportunity slip. Not only will she benefit by it, he will make some money out of it as well. She tells him, 'You've grown greedy for money, Dulan, you're not thinking about me.

Bikhni isn't here, how can I go alone to mourn?' He suggests that she gather prostitutes from Tohri, from the whore's quarter. 'And then your Parbatia is there as well.' Sanichari asks, 'I? Go to the whore's quarter? To Parbatia?' 'For the sake of money you can do anything,' counters Dulan. Note the shift in emphasis from the stomach/food to money: perhaps a slight slippage, but one which signifies very differently. Throughout the original, the stomach/hunger/food is used as the basic term indicating survival. Money, after all, is one step removed, one transaction further up from the bottom line. Food equates directly with survival. Money signifies food and therefore survival, but it also signifies possessions, for example, or power. As a metaphor for survival it is more compromised than the stomach is.

Dulan informs Sanichari that Gambhir Singh himself had wanted the randis (whores) to act as rudalis at his funeral. Sanichari says, 'He expects the very women whose lives he ruined to cry over his corpse?!' Dulan chides her, 'Don't concern yourself with all that! Just think about your own business.' The words used, 'kaam-dhanda', literally mean the business one does to earn money. The admonition has the effect of divorcing her own personal financial considerations from a more general interest in the randis' motives, or the ironic implications of their mourning for the man who has ruined them.

After he exits, Bikhni's nephew comes on with the news of her death. As in the story, Sanichari's outward reaction is very stoic, controlled. She asks a few questions and then dismisses the boy. Alone, she picks up an item of clothing belonging to Bikhni, and then breaks down. Grating sobs tear through her, rending the silence. Her mourning is done in complete privacy, all the more poignant when contrasted with the sham display of public mourning which is a form of commercial exchange. The story very clearly states that Sanichari does not cry, although she is devastated with grief. She recognizes that she feels fear, identifies why, and then gets up to go and consult Dulan. She acts. Here, the emphasis shifts from fear to sorrow, in keeping with the central importance given to the Sanichari-Bikhni relationship. But here, too, the scene does not close on the tears. We see her through the despair to some form of acceptance, as she gets up and replaces Bikhni's clothing from where she lifted it.

Survival despite despair, is the message of the play. Survival through struggle, is the central message of the story.

Scene eleven is situated in the prostitutes' quarters of Tohri. Colour, music, noise, a community of women engaged in various pursuits identified with the feminine: applying nail polish, massaging a baby with oil. In order to get the ambience and details correct, Usha Ganguli visited the redlight district on an observation mission (more about that later). After allowing us a glimpse of the 'off-duty' life of these women—marked by the same kind of petty quarrelling and accusations of pilfering that mark community life in the village—Sanichari enters, asking for Parbatia, who turns hostile as soon as she recognizes her mother-in-law. Sanichari says, and repeats, that she is here to 'help' them. This is untrue. We already know that she is here, reluctantly, because she needs *their* help, not vice versa. This untruth immediately makes her relationship to these women asymmetrical. The condescension and unequal equation implied contradicts the story which projects the prostitutes as equals and co-victims and talks of mutual co-operation as opposed to the 'decent' women setting out to 'help' the fallen women. In the story Sanichari matter-of-factly tells them that when they grow old and can't work as prostitutes they can work as rudalis, and offers to initiate them into the profession while she's still around. At no point does she imply that the latter profession is in any way 'better' than the former. Nor does she bring up the concept of izzat (self-respect) with all its accompanying baggage of moral and social judgements and patriarchal formulations, as she does in the play. After Parbatia rejects her out of hand, saying she refuses to cry over the corpses of the very men who have used and abused them, Sanichari turns to the other women. It is interesting that, unlike in the story, here the women need convincing about becoming rudalis. Perhaps this is done to create the forum for a debate, with pros and cons being presented. Parbatia's reason can be classified as an 'ethical' one. Next comes a 'practical' one—why should they give up a steady daily income for a less steady job? After all, deaths don't occur every day. There is insecurity involved—the job may be here today, gone tomorrow. Sanichari does not counter Parbatia's 'ethical' objection by asserting, as she does in the story, that they can use this job as a means of revenge. But she rebuts each of the 'practical' arguments one by one. They don't earn enough as prostitutes to fill their stomachs, nor do they retain their self-respect. 'No clothes, no food, no self-respect.' What do they gain? And as for insecurity—'You're still young today—what happens tomorrow? Look, this is work, you hear me? Work. Better work than yours. Hard work like grinding grain in the chakki, splitting logs of wood, digging the earth.' Once again this contradicts the story, which does not draw a moral distinction between the labour of prostitution and 'honest hard work.' In fact, the story repeatedly stresses that all forms of work are equal: mourning, prostitution, working in the fields; each is a way of keeping the stomach fed.

Slowly the women begin to show an interest, assuring themselves that the pay is adequate, that they'll get clothing and food, enquiring if there are any brothers or nephews who might be potential clients, and so on. Gulbadan announces that she, for one, cannot resist the revenge of 'mourning' the death of her father, the man who ruined her mother and her. By the end of the scene they are all clustered around Sanichari, with only Parbatia noticeably aloof, refusing to be drawn in to the community.

The twelfth and final scene begins with the funeral of Gambhir Singh and the thakurs paying their last respects to the rotting corpse lying in state. The stink pervades the gathering, and this olfactory metaphor for something rotten in the system complements the hypocrisy of the scene. The band of rudalis enters, announcing its arrival with a loud chorus of lamentation. They launch into a tightly choreographed, highly stylized performance in perfect unison. During this, Gulbadan makes eye contact with Madho Singh, who reciprocates. Gulbadan and Madho Singh come together, seem to strike a deal, and slip away. The stage empties. Sanichari is left standing alone. Dulan enters and hands her a bundle, saying that this is payment in kind, and that cash will follow. He exits. The focus is on Sanichari, solitary again as she was in the beginning, a scarred survivor.

The original story closes on the upbeat. Sanichari is positive, the prostitutes are having a good time, and Gulbadan's sneering wink at her 'cousin' is much more equivocal than the come-on we see in the play. There is a distinct feeling of an encounter, with the round going to the rudalis; of a skirmish which is won by the women. The story ends on a note of triumph. The opposite is true of the play. The subversive connotations of the rudali custom are not developed in the play. There is a tremendous sense of drama in the stylized sequence where the rudalis perform, but it does not include any irony. Sanichari's stance is one of stoic resignation. She has survived, but there is no sense of triumph or victory. She remains, as she was at the beginning, lonely, burdened, unloved. In the original we see a definite evolution in Sanichari, leaving her stronger, freer and more in control of her situation. The trajectory in the play is very different. The middle of the play, Bikhni's presence in her life, lifts her out of loneliness, but at the end she is back where she started. She knows she will survive. But survival at such cost feels like defeat.

III

As we study the minutiae of microlevel changes within scenes, patterns emerge. These change-patterns group themselves around basic shifts in perception and agenda. Let us identify the main differences of emphasis and direction between the play and the original text.

One category of changes clusters around Usha Ganguli's gendered perception of 'Rudali' as a woman's story. In the play Sanichari is constructed as the central character, and the entire text is her story. It opens and closes with her, and she is present in every scene. Tightly constructed, the movement of the play is to first establish the harsh, poverty-ridden situation of her life, then her solitude as one by one her family drops away, then the discovery of caring and friendship through Bikhni with, for the first time, companionship, cemented through the new profession they adopt as rudalis, then the return to solitude and finally the realization that life goes on and one survives. The original, as we have seen, does not privilege the story of Sanichari to the same degree. Her life is woven into the fabric of a larger socio-economic critique.

In the play Sanichari, from the beginning, is a matriarch, a woman of agency. Usha Ganguli comments on the feminist connotations of this: 'In our Indian society men see women . . . from a different point of view. For them

Sanichari's character would have been very weak, very soft, helpless. They would have made her a victim. Sanichari is very hardworking, there is no doubt of that. But she is not a helpless victim.'[1] In effect, the figure of Sanichari in the play—longsuffering, enduring, stoic—echoes the seminal Mother Courage,[2] a theatre image comfortable and familiar to urban audiences who have seen her reincarnated in many languages. This idea of Woman as noble survivor, in fact, fits more easily into a tradition of perceiving Woman as victimized. The story, on the other hand, details a gradual evolution to empowerment. The process of constructing Sanichari as a figure of authority in the play, as the provider and decision-maker in her home, has a reductive effect on the familial and community male-female relationships which are sympathetically developed in detail in the original story, such as Sanichari's relationships with her husband (absent from the play), her son and Dulan ganju.

Sensitively depicted, strongly acted, the relationship between the two peers, Bikhni and Sanichari, makes a powerful feminist statement about female bonding. The play develops it with a slight but telling shift in focus, with that one intimate scene of physical and emotional tenderness. Moroever, by isolating and detailing this single close relationship in Sanichari's life, its centrality is highlighted—it is the emotional focus of the play. The story balances it against the other closenesses Sanichari has experienced, with her husband, and, more foregrounded, with her son.

The subject of prostitutes is treated with interesting differences in the two texts. Both include the community and profession of prostitutes within the space of the narrative, but they are imaged differently. The play presents them as bold, earthy and energetic, not suffering victims. Yet it also slips in the question of social-moral acceptability by raising the issue of izzat, positioning 'decent' women versus 'indecent' ones. Sanichari argues in the play that the profession of rudali is 'better' than that of prostitution; by urging them to switch she is improving their lot. The entire argument by which Sanichari persuades the prostitutes to become rudalis assumes

---

1. Interview with Usha Ganguly on 22.4.93
2. Bertolt Brecht, *Mother Courage*, one of his most widely performed and translated plays.

that they have to make a choice. This assumption is posited on the belief that women employed in a 'decent' profession cannot work alongside 'indecent' prostitutes. This is completely opposed to the story, where it is quite clear that the women, including Sanichari and Bikhni, do other kinds of work round the year, and act as rudalis only when the occasion arises—in other words, one can be both a prostitute and a rudali, and there is no contradiction between the two means of livelihood. The story strongly presents prostitutes as the victims of a system, poor, exploited, struggling to feed themselves, just like the other villagers. Any immorality or social shame associated with them exists only in the eyes of the upper classes, who are held responsible for their condition anyway.

No doubt both the author of the story and the auteur of the production equally feel that hers is the more 'realistic' stance—as no doubt each is, the former in the rural, the latter in the urban middle-class context. Usha Ganguli explains that she feels it unrealistic that prostitutes would give up their profession to become rudalis ('In the last sequence we see that . . . one of them leaves the group to go off with a man. They have a profession, they cannot just become rudalis overnight! This is life, and . . . realism.'[1]). She obviously sees prostitution and funeral wailing as mutually exclusive professions. This is an urban understanding: prostitutes are a separate community; their rural linkages and family histories are rendered invisible to the urban gaze once they leave their village homes, remaining visible only to themselves. The story presents no such dichotomy.

Another category of changes clusters around Usha Ganguli's perception of what constitutes 'reality'. Like Mahasweta Devi, she is firm in her rejection of any romanticization or sentimentalization of the treatment: 'I didn't want to treat this story in a sentimental way and make it a mere melodrama.'[2] In that sense both texts adopt a non-idealized approach. But Mahasweta Devi's portrayal of community and her resolution of her text seem idealized to Usha Ganguli's urban sensibilities. She prefers to present both positive and negative characters, does not reconcile Sanichari

---

1. Interview with Usha Ganguli on 20.4.93
2. Ibid.

and Parbatia at the end, and shows Gulbadan as soliciting clients in the midst of her rudali performance ('I was very disturbed about the ending of the play. Mahasweta di's story ends in idealism . . . but I felt that this was not real, this was not how things happen in life.'[1]

With both Mahasweta Devi and Usha Ganguli using the yardstick of 'realism' to measure their texts, the question of whose perception is more 'realistic' emphasizes the provisional nature of that term itself. Both study detail and fact—and then present them as part of their own agenda. Mahasweta Devi's experience of the rural condition is the base of what she writes about; her choice of what to depict and how to depict it is ideologically motivated. Her writing is activist; and her stance is unequivocal. She has taken sides, and declared it, and her fiction takes sides as well. The illusory stance of 'objectivity' is totally irrelevant to her writing. Not so with the playtext. Usha Ganguli has her own agenda. She aims to present a powerful tale of the harsh reality of a woman's life in rural India, a tale of struggle and survival. But other media shape and filter her knowledge of that 'reality' rather than firsthand experience. She feels obliged to take a more 'objective', non-'idealized' stance from her less engaged urban position, to build an image of reality which her urban audience will have no hesitation in accepting as authentic. This includes an invented language (a pseudo-dialect was constructed which would be both understandable to an urban audience, and yet convey the 'feel' of a rural language) and shifts of characterization, and is an urbanized construct which functions from an position of sympathy, not active engagement.

A third category of changes coheres around Usha Ganguli's choice of medium and genre. At this stage of her theatre activity she believed that social realism and proscenium theatre was the most effective and powerful form, and the one she preferred to use. Drawing on close observation she suggests the material details of a particular social setting to create an impression of realism. She constructs a strong storyline with a definite beginning, middle and end. Each scene is carefully balanced between stillness and action. Visual and aural motifs are woven

---

1 Interview with Usha Ganguli on 20.4.93.

through the text (the chakki, for example). The dull colours of costumes and sets are interspersed with vivid, colourful settings for dramatic contrast and tension (the mela, the funerals, the randipatti). Sequences of stylization integrate with and highlight by contrast the naturalism of the acting and movement, as in the tightly choreographed mourning sequence at the end of the play. Usha Ganguli's priority is to create good theatre—meaningful, and therefore the content is important—but above all, emotionally powerful, gripping theatre, directed at an urban audience. She constructs her text and her production to that end. Mahasweta Devi's priority is activist intervention, through her writing, in the struggle of the tribals, bonded labour and rural dispossessed she works amidst. She constructs her fiction to that end.

What does this detailed mapping of shifts and divergences signify other than that two individuals have created two differing texts? To begin with, Mahasweta Devi is one of our most important writers, not least because she happens to be a woman, involved in work which fuses her activism and her creative writing. She has managed to suture the split between these two fields of activity so that, as she says, her work as activist, journalist/editor and creative writer complement one another and overlap. She inscribes the discourse of gender within that of class without in any way reducing or devaluing the former's significance; and 'Rudali', though written from a 'class point of view' as she says, is an important feminist text, making important feminist statements.

Usha Ganguli has established a reputation for serious theatre work, both as a director and as an actress. Committed to what she calls 'serious, meaningful' theatre in Hindi in an urban situation, she has directed plays with large all-male casts and themes which do not attempt to foreground women's issues. This is the first time she has addressed a text which, as she sees it, has for its subject the Indian woman. Her play *Rudali* is also a powerful women's text which communicates a feminist message.

Apart from the confusion and ambiguity surrounding the umbrella term 'feminism' itself (discussed at the beginning of this paper) there are deeper tensions fissuring the field of 'feminist' awareness and engagement. The divide between activists and theorists/writers/intellectuals is one of them. The divide between rural and urban perspectives is another. That between differing politics and ideologies is a third; that between the upper and middle-classes and lower classes a fourth. The result is many differing forms and directions of feminist activity, one could say many differing feminisms.

In this context The metamorphosis of 'Rudali' is uniquely significant because it foregrounds these differences. Here we have two important women practitioners in the field of cultural production, who see themselves as progressive, and who are responsible for works which are widely perceived as feminist—or, if one quarrels with that term, as important from a woman's perspective. We see how their texts are shaped by an agenda, by priorities which are in turn determined by a basic ideological position and by the purpose of the text: in one case, activist intervention, in the other, performance for an urban audience. The metamorphosis of 'Rudali' allows us to address the simultaneity and asymmetry of feminist stances and positions in this country today.

Rudali[1]

Mahasweta Devi

IN TAHAD VILLAGE, ganjus and dushads were in the majority.[2] Sanichari was a ganju by caste. Like the other villagers, her life too was lived in desperate poverty. Her mother-in-law used to say it was because Sanichari was born on inauspicious Saturday that her destiny was full of suffering. At that time Sanichari was a young daughter-in-law; she wasn't free to speak up. Her mother-in-law died when Sanichari was still young. She was never able to answer back. Sometimes the old woman's words came back to Sanichari. To herself she would say—Huh! Because I was born on and named after a Saturday, that made me an unlucky daughter-in-law! You were born on a Monday—was your life any happier? Somri, Budhua, Moongri, Bishri[3]—do any of them have happier lives?

When her mother-in-law died Sanichari didn't cry. At the time, her husband and his brother, both the old

1. From Mahasweta Devi, Nairetey Megh (Calcutta: Karuna Prakashini, 1980).
2. 'Untouchable' castes.
3. Like Sanichari, which comes from Sanichar or Saturday, these are names derived from days of the week: Somri from Som (Monday), Budhua from Budh (Wednesday), Moongri from Mangal (Tuesday) and Bishri from Brihaspati (Thursday).

woman's sons, were in jail because of malik-mahajan Ramavatar Singh.[1] Enraged at the loss of some wheat, he had all the young dushad and ganju males of the village locked up. Her mother-in-law died in great pain, of dropsy, lying in her own excrement, crying out, over and over, 'food, give me food!'. It was pouring that night. Sanichari and her sister-in-law together lowered the old woman on to the ground. If the rites weren't carried out before the night was over, they would have to bear the cost of the repentance rites for keeping the corpse in the house overnight. And there wasn't even a cupful of grain in the house! So Sanichari was forced to go from neighbour to neighbour in the pouring rain. Dragging the neighbours home with her, and handling all the arrangements for the cremation, she was so busy that there was no time to cry. So what if there wasn't? The old woman had given her so much trouble that even if Sanichari had tried to cry she wouldn't have been able to wring out many tears.

The old woman couldn't stand being alone while she was alive. She couldn't stand being alone after death either. Within three years the brother-in-law and his wife were dead too. At that time Ramavatar Singh had started a hue and cry about throwing the dushads and ganjus out of the village. Terrified of being driven out, Sanichari was on tenterhooks. There was no crying over those deaths either. Was one to weep or to worry about how to burn the corpses and feed the neighbours cheaply at the shradh?[2] In this village everyone is unhappy. They understand suffering. So they are content with being fed just sour curd, sugar and coarse parched rice. Everyone understands the fact that Sanichari and her husband don't shed any tears—how is it possible to weep? when you've borne three deaths in as many years? Their grief must have hardened into stone within them! To herself, Sanichari had sighed with relief. Is it possible to feed so many mouths on the meagre scrapings they bring home after labouring on the malik's field? Two dead, just as well. At least their own stomachs would be full.

She had never thought, however, that she wouldn't cry at her husband's death. And yet, such was her destiny, that

---

1. Landlord-moneylender.
2. A funeral ceremony.

this was just what happened. At the time her only son, Budhua, was six. Leaving the little child at home, Sanichari laboured hard for the sake of a little security in her household. She would go off to the malik's house where she would split wood, gather fodder for the cows, and in harvest season work alongside her husband in the fields. A piece of land had been left to her husband's brother by her father-in-law; together the couple had built a little hut on it. She had painted designs and pictures on the walls. Budhua's father wanted to fence in their angan,[1] and grow chillies and vegetables. She had plans to raise a calf she would get from the malik's wife. It was all fixed. Her husband said, Come, let's visit the Baisakhi mela at Tohri.[2] We can offer worship to Shiva as well. After all, we've managed to save up seven rupees!

The mela was a grand affair. The Shiva idol was being bathed in pots and pots of milk donated by the rich. This milk had been collecting in large tanks over the past few days. It gave off a sour stink, and was thick with buzzing flies. People were paying the pandas[3] money to drink glasses of this milk and promptly falling sick with cholera. Many died. Including Budhua's father. It was during British rule. Government officials were dragging the victims off to the hospital tents. There were only five tents. There were sixty to seventy patients. The tents were cordoned off with barbed wire. Sanichari and her son sat and waited beyond the barbed wire. They came to know that Budhua's father had died. The government officers didn't give her any time to shed tears. They burned the corpses quickly. They dragged Sanichari and Budhua off for a vaccination against the disease. The pain of the injection made them howl. Still crying, she washed off the sindoor from her head in the shallow Kuruda river, broke her bangles, and returned to the village.[4] They were new shellac bangles. She had just bought them at the fair. The panda of the Shiva temple at Tohri demanded that she make ritual offerings there before returning to her village, since her husband had died there.

---

1. Courtyard.
2. A fair held to celebrate the Hindu New Year.
3. Lower-order priests who act as guides to pilgrims.
4. Vermilion (sindoor) in the parting of the hair is a sign of marriage; therefore, wiping it off and breaking one's bangles is a ritual of widowhood.

On his insistence she spent a precious rupee and a quarter on a spartan offering of sand and sattu which Budhua offered as pinda.[1] But what a to-do there was over this when she got back to her village! Mohanlal, the priest of Ramavatar's presiding deity, scoffed—what! A mere offering of sand, that too in river water! Is Budhua Lord Ramachandra, repeating His act of offering a pinda of sand for His father, King Dasharatha![2]

But the priest said . . .

Can a Tohri brahmin know how a Tahad villager's kriya is done?[3] By obeying him you've insulted your local priest!

In order to appease Mohanlal she was forced into debt to Ramavatar—she received Rs 20 and put her thumbprint on a paper stating that she would repay Rs 50 through bonded labour on his fields over the next 5 years—and after paying for Budhua's father's shradh, she was so hardpressed to feed her little son, that she never had time to cry for her husband. One day, in the hard heat of summer, as she laboured in Ramavatar's field, she threw down her implements and stalked off to the shade of a peepul tree. She told her fellow labourers, today I'm going to cry my heart out for Budhua's father. I'm going to cry good and hard.

Why are you going to cry today? Dulan ganju asks.

You'll all go home with wages to show for your labour. I'm slaving to repay a debt. I'll go home with a handful of sattu—that's why I'll cry. Haven't I reason enough?

So that's the real reason for your crying. Why drag your dead husband into it?

You're a real so-and-so, Latua's father.

Have you calculated? A year has passed already.

A full year!

Yes.

He's been gone a whole year?

Time passes on an empty stomach.

---

1. Sattu is flour, usually made from gram, a cheap but nourishing food eaten by the poor. Pinda is the ritual offering made by the offspring for the peace of the departed parent's soul.
2. The reference is to an incident in the epic Ramayana, in which Rama, exiled to the forest, makes the required offering for the soul of his departed father the king with the means at hand: a fistful of sand washed by river water.
3. A funeral ceremony.

If only I could die!

And if you did, what would happen to your son Budhua? Don't talk nonsense. Now see here—so what if you've signed yourself into debt? Look at me. I do my work slowly, slowly. The longer I take, the longer I earn a daily wage. Why are you killing yourself over that bastard's fields? Take it easy. As long as there's work, there's something for the stomach.

That day, too, Sanichari didn't cry.

Everyone notices everything in the village. There was plenty of talk about the fact that Sanichari hadn't wept and mourned. She paid it no attention. Her debt to Ramavatar Singh was not paid off and might never have been. But at the time Sanichari was looking after a black calf. Ashrafi's mother left it in her care while she was visiting Gaya. Ramavatar Singh's uncle was on his deathbed, and this calf's tail was placed in the dying man's hand to help him cross the Baitarani river into the afterlife.[1] Sanichari saw that the room was full of people. All Ramavatar's peers and kin were there. She suddenly thought of a scheme. From outside the door she loudly pleaded, You who are the benefactor of the poor! This poor woman begs you to reward the service she did you today! Please wipe out the debt due! Write it off as repaid!

Ramavatar would be gaining fifty bighas of prime land thanks to his uncle's death. Who knows why he agreed to Sanichari's request. Later he had to face a lot of criticism for this act. The other jotedars[2] and mahajans claimed that ever since he agreed to wipe out the debt, the untouchable fieldhands had started getting above themselves. It was not the amount that mattered—that was of less value than the dust off their shoes. What mattered was the yoke, the burden of debt that kept them labouring like cattle.

Ramavatar would reply, my uncle was dying, my mind was heavy with sorrow, I was feeling very low. I felt that I should give away everything to anyone who wanted it, and become a sanyasi.[3]

When his son Lachman got married, he extracted the expense of the musicians from Sanichari and her people.

---

1. Mythical river that separates this world from the other.
2. Landholders
3. An ascetic who has renounced worldly attachments.

Preoccupied with all this, and with ways of keeping the stomach fed, Sanichari forgot to cry. Budhua grew up. Like his father, he took the yoke of poverty onto his shoulders. He had got married years ago. His bride now came to set up house. They had a son. She was like a daini.[1] Through her contacts in the marketplace she managed to feed herself on all sorts of stuff. Day by day she prospered and grew bigger and bigger. While hauling sacks of wheat for Ramavatar's son Lachman, Budhua contracted the wasting fever and hacking cough of tuberculosis. The fever rises at night, then breaks in a sweat at dawn. There is blood when he coughs, dark shadows under his eyes. Sanichari felt as if the flames of the funeral pyre were burning within her, she felt the scorching heat blowing about her day and night. She could see that he was going to die, and realized that her dreams of building a life around Budhua would never be fulfilled. Even her more modest dreams have never been realized. She had wanted to buy a wooden comb for her hair, to wear shellac bangles for a full year—neither of these dreams had materialized. With time, her dreams had changed shape. Her son and daughter-in-law would earn enough, they would support her, she imagined sitting in the winter sun sharing a bowl of gur[2] and sattu with her grandson—Had this last dream been over-ambitious? Had she sinned by wanting too much? Is that why Budhua was wasting away before her eyes?

Sanichari was unable to scold or reprimand her daughter-in-law. How could she speak harshly to Budhua's wife, the mother of her grandson? Budhua understood. One day he said—Ma, don't say anything to her.

To whom?

To your daughter-in-law.

Why d'you bring this up?

Budhua smiled wanly. He said—Ma, she steals from the money she makes selling vegetables, to buy stuff to eat. I know this. She does it out of hunger, ma.

Don't I feed her?

Her hunger is greater, ma.

People talk.

Yes, I know. I know why they talk. But I don't

---

1. Term for women who are deemed witches.
2. Jaggery.

want to discuss this any more. How is she to know, ma, how you and I have struggled to build this little household—

He started to cough. Rubbing his chest, Sanichari said, I've stopped calling upon god. If there was a god, your sickness would have come to me instead.

No, ma. If you live, my son will live.

And if I want my son to live?

Sanichari beat her forehead, decrying her fate. Budhua has brought their angan alive. Okra, eggplant, radish, chillies, pumpkin. A variety of vegetables. With seeds and cuttings from Lachman's garden, he has nurtured his vegetable patch. His wife is plump. She is always hungry. She begged to be allowed to work in Lachman's fields. She never seems to get enough. That way she could feed herself. Budhua heard her out, then told her—Wait till the child is born. After that, I'll arrange things the way you want.

He really worked hard. He fenced in the yard with thornbush and dug the soil. He sneaked in manure from Lachman's fields. He carried water from the river. Within a few months the angan was blooming. Sanichari smiled delightedly, Well done, Budhua! Your father had wanted to plant a vegetable patch just like this!

The grandchild was born. When he was a month-and-a-half old, the wife began to insist on going to work. Budhua told her, Sure. You can take the vegetables to market to sell. But I won't let you work in the malik's fields. Young women who work for him never return home.

Why, where do they go?

First to a nice house, then to the randipatti—the whores' quarters. If you bring up the subject again, I'll knock your head off.

She went to market.

Sanichari asked, You sent her to the market, Budhua? She could have stayed at home, I'd have gone instead.

No, ma, When you and I slogged in the fields, she stayed at home. Did she ever cook, clean, fetch water?

No.

Both mother and son knew that she would never be content with an ailing husband, a poverty-stricken existence. Sanichari told her—He hasn't got long to live. The signs of death are on his face. As long as he's alive, please behave yourself.

She obeyed this request to the letter. She stayed exactly as long as he was alive. The child was six months old at the time. That day—not just that day, for several days before that—Budhua's condition had worsened. The vaid's medicine was not working.[1] Sanichari asked her to stay with Budhua. She herself went, running all the way she went, to ask the vaid for some other medicine. She went even though she knew that no medicine could help him now. The vaid's house was about a mile away. How on earth did she manage to run all that way? But the vaid was not home, he was at the market. When he got back, she began pestering him for medicine. He was annoyed and said, The lower castes have no patience, no ability to bear up. If the boy's condition is so serious, why is his wife on her way to the marketplace? Your son must be okay.

Sanichari got home to find her son dead and her daughter-in-law gone. The baby was crying in the room.

Her bahu never returned.[2] With the child in her arms she busied herself cremating Budhua and fending off queries about her bahu. In all this, she didn't cry for her son either. Nor could she cry. She would sit, like one stunned; then fall into exhausted slumber.

Village people are continually caught up in squabbles and quarrels. After Budhua's death, Sanichari saw another side to them. She was in upto her neck looking after Haroa, the baby. So much so that she seemed to forget that Budhua was no more. She couldn't remember a time when he wasn't there with her. While she slaved in the malik-mahajan's fields, he would clean the house and fetch water from the river. He would take grains of wheat and corn scavenged from the dusty fields, and wash them clean in the river. Gentle, quiet, understanding—the son of a suffering mother. How could she accept that she would never again have to warm water for him at night, or rub him down with the auspicious swapnadya ointment which promised relief?[3] Budhua's son

1. Practitioner of traditional medicine.
2. Daughter-in-law, wife.
3. 'Swapnadya' means 'seen in one's dreams'. This denotes a supernatural, auspicious quality to the item thus dreamt of: in this case a magical cure-all

would cry and cry.

One day Dulan's wife, Dhatua and Latua's mother, notorious for her badtempered and quarrelsome ways, came by. She picked up the baby and cradled him.

What are you doing, eh, Dhatua's mother?

Let me take Haroa with me.

Why?

Dhatua's wife is nursing a child. He'll drink her milk.

Why? He's my grandchild. I'll bring him up.

We all bring up our own children and grand-children. So will you. But Dhatua's father said to tell you, there's a job going.

Where?

The *gormen* is repairing the *rail-line*.[1] Dhatua's father has a contract to supply 20 labourers.

Aren't you going?

Our cow's with calf. Plus there's a puja in the malik's house. Clearing land, splitting firewood—lots of obligatory work to be done.

That Dulan ganju—one helluva smart old so-and-so! He's trapping me into working again!

That's upto you.

The breastfeeding by Dhatua's wife kept Haroa alive. While Sanichari worked on the job, she didn't need to cook. Dulan's wife would send her meal of roti and achar along with Dulan's.[2] Sanichari repaid the debt of wheatflour. But there are some debts that can never be repaid.

Dulan and his family looked out for her, and Parbhu ganju said, You're completely alone now. You're like an aunt to me, why don't you shift your hut into my yard?

Natua dushad sold her vegetables for her in the market. If her fellow-villagers had not rallied around in this manner, would Sanichari have survived? No one mentioned that Budhua's wife's had become a whore. Still, Sanichari found out that she had run away with a medicineman who hawked cheap remedies from fair to fair, and who had promised to show her towns like Gaya, Ara, Bhagalpur, to

---

ointment.
1. 'Gormen' (government) and 'rail-line' are in English in the original.
2. Unleavened bread and pickle.

take her to dances, cinemas, circuses, to feast her on puri and kachauri every day.[1]

Why didn't she take her son with her?

A childhood memory of Moti's mother came to Sanichari's mind. The malik had wanted to keep Moti, but her mother refused. Then Moti ran away with the rail-line construction contractor. When Moti's mother would come to grind wheat on Sanichari's mother's grindstone she would say—if I had handed Moti over to the malik, at least I would have got to see her now and then.

Sanichari does not feel that way. Since she's gone, it's better that she's lost to them for good. Otherwise, she'd be queening it in the malik's house. Sanichari and Haroa would be slaving away outside. That would be very humiliating. Moreover, Sanichari knows from experience that the people of the village would shun her totally. Which would make it impossible for her to live in the village. In order to survive, the poor and oppressed need the support of the other poor and oppressed. Without that support, it is impossible to live in the village even on milk and ghee provided by the malik.[2]

Slowly Sanichari felt normal again. She brought up Haroa as best she could. The community elders would often tell Haroa—your grandmother has suffered a lot. Don't you give her trouble now.

Haroa would listen to all this with his head bowed. When he turned fourteen Sanichari took him to the new malik-mahajan Lachman Singh, the son of Ramavatar Singh. Times have changed, and the maliks have changed with the times. Lachman Singh now employed musclemen to keep the labourers, lower castes and peasants in line; mounted, armed musclemen. Ramavatar was given to kicking and beating them with his slipper, but when in a good mood he would also chat with them. To Lachman Singh, this was a sign of weakness. He preferred to keep his distance.

Sanichari approached Lachman Singh, saying—You know all there is to know about my situation. There is no one more unfortunate than I am. This is my grandson. Please find some work for him. Otherwise, how will we survive?

Perhaps Lachman Singh was in a good mood at the

---

1. Deep-fried snacks made of flour, sometimes stuffed.
2. Milk and clarified butter—the height of luxury.

time. He said—The boy can work in my shop in the market-place, carrying goods and doing the sweeping and cleaning. He'll get Rs 2 a month and his meals.

Huzoor's kindness![1]

Sanichari and her grandson got up and left. Sanichari prepared a talisman for him with prasad[2] she got from Mohanlal, and tied the charm around his neck, talking to him all the while.

The marketplace is full of buffaloes. Don't go there, Haroa. If one kicks you, you could die.

Yes, Nani.

Don't pay attention to what wicked people say.

No, Nani.

The boy worked hard for the first few months. He would hand over his pay to his grandmother. He would carry his ration of sattu and gur home. In time he began to fill out, look better. Gradually he grew bored and restless. Once he didn't bring home his pay, he bought a coloured vest instead. Another time he bought a plastic mouth organ. Sanichari created quite a to-do. Then Lachman informed her that Haroa wasn't working at the shop, he spent his time following the magic-show fellows around. This time Sanichari gave him a thrashing. She warned him that if he misbehaved she would cut off his foot, confine him to the house and feed him if necessary, but she wouldn't let him stray from the right path.

After that Haroa put his mind to his job for a while. Then he ran away. Natua came and told her—Haroa has run away with the magic-show lot.

Let him go.

But Sanichari didn't let it go at that. She went from one marketplace to another, from one fairground to another, looking for him. It didn't occur to her to cry for him. It felt as if this was bound to happen. Then, when she had given up hope of recovering Haroa, suddenly she met Bikhni. Bikhni was a childhood playmate. Everyone called her Kalikambli Bikhni because she always wore a ghagra made out of a black quilt.[3] Carrying a bundle on her shoulder she was striding

---

1. Huzoor is a term of respect, equivalent to 'sir' or 'master'.
2. Food offerings, once blessed and consecrated by the gods to whom they are offered in worship, are called prasad. They are distributed to devotees after the prayer ceremony.
3. Kalikambli implies 'black-quilted'. A ghagra is a traditional gathered

along hastily. Not noticing Sanichari, she bumped into her.

What the hell? Are you blind?

It's your father who's blind.

What did you say?

You heard me all right.

A fine fight was brewing. Sanichari was all set to enjoy herself. A good set-to cleared the brain, got rid of a lot of undergrowth. That's why Dhatua's mother literally quarrelled with the crows—quarrelling kept both mind and body in fine fettle, the blood coursing through your veins like bullets from a gun. But as they glared at each other, Bikhni asked—Hey, aren't you Sanichari?

Who're you?

Bikhni. Kalikambli Bikhni.

Bikhni?

Yes!

But you were married off in Lohardaga.

I've been living in Jujubhatu for many years.

Jujubhatu? And I've been in Tahad, just half a day's walk from you! How come we never met?

Come, let's sit down somewhere.

They settled down in the shade of a peepul tree. They eyed each other closely, before each relaxed in the realization that the other was no better off than herself. Like Sanichari, Bikhni's wrists, throat and forehead sport no jewellery other than blue tattoo marks, both wear pieces of cork in their ears instead of earrings, their hair is rough and ungroomed. Sanichari handed Bikhni a bidi.[1]

Did you come to the market?

No, I came to look for my grandson.

Sanichari told her about Haroa, about herself, about everything. Bikhni listened, then said—Is there no caring left in this world? Or is it just our fate, yours and mine?

Sanichari laughed bitterly—No husband, no son, wherever my grandson is, may he be safe.

Bikhni said—I had a son after three daughters. Their father died long ago, I was the one who brought him up. I began to take in calves for rearing, and gradually I managed four cows, and two she-goats of my own. I got my son

---

skirt.
1. A cheap indigenous smoke.

married, and I fed the whole village on dahi-chivda-gur[1] after taking a loan from the mahajan.

Then?

Now the mahajan is about to claim my house by way of repayment, and my son is moving in with his in-laws.

Bikhni spat while saying this. She said, His father-in-law has no sons. My son will live there along with his brothers-in-law as his servant. I told him, let's sell the cows and repay the debt to the mahajan, but my son took the cows and calves away to his in-laws. But I am Bikhni, after all. I've just sold my two goats in this marketplace. My son doesn't know. *Bas*, I've got twenty rupees in the tank, and I'm off.

Where will you go now?

Who knows? Your son's no more, mine's as good as dead. Perhaps I'll go to Daltonganj, or Bokharo or Gomo. Beg on some station.

Sanichari heaved a sigh. She said, Come with me. My two-roomed hut is empty. Each room has a platform to sleep on. Budhua built them. The vegetable patch still yields okra, eggplant, chillies.

And when my money runs out?

We'll face that when it happens. Your money is yours. Sanichari can still earn enough to subsist on.

Then let's go. Tell me, is there a water problem in your village?

There's the river. And the panchayati well,[2] though that water's bitter.

Just a minute.

Bikhni went back to the market and returned after a short while. She said, I've bought some medicine for lice. We'll mix it with kerosene and massage it in, then wash our hair. Lice can worry you more than the most worrying thoughts!

Walking along, Bikhni said, My grand-daughter will probably cry for me. She's used to sleeping beside me.

Sanichari said, Only for a few days. Then she'll forget.

---

1. Yoghurt, flattened rice and jaggery.
2. Panchayat: system of village- and district-level self-government; the well dug by the panchayat.

Bikhni was delighted with Sanichari's house. Right then and there she sprinkled the place with water and washed it down. She went off to the river and fetched a pot of water. She said, there's no need to light the stove tonight. I have some roti and achar with me.

Bikhni loved housework. Within a couple of days, she had put a fresh coat of mud and dung on the floor of the house and compound, washed Sanichari's and her own clothes thoroughly, aired all the mats and quilts. At home, she had withdrawn more and more from the housework as her daughter-in-law took the reins into her own hands. This was out of hurt pride, but her daughter-in-law thought she was lazy. Managing a household is addictive. It can set even someone as unhappy as Bikhni to dreaming unrealistic dreams. There's no knowing how long she'll be here—this is Sanichari's house. One day Bikhni began to dig and tend the vegetable patch. She said, With a little effort we'll get lots of vegetables.

The lice medicine killed the creatures in Sanichari's hair. After sleeping comfortably she realized that her sleepless nights had been caused by the lice, not mental anguish. No matter how griefstricken one is, a work-worn body is bound to sleep well.

For some days the two of them ate off Bikhni's money. When that ran out, Sanichari felt as if the sky had fallen on her head. That very day, a wolf took away one of Dulan's calves. While they were all abustle with chasing away this wolf, they received news that the corpse of a local jotedar, Bhairab Singh, had been found murdered by someone or a group of people. His body was found lying in one of his fields over which there had been a court dispute for a while. Now it would be upgraded to a criminal case. The villagers always come to know everything. They soon knew that it was Bhairab Singh's eldest son who had killed him. He was worried by his father's excessive affection for his sons by a second marriage. He now threatened to charge his stepbrothers with murder. In turn, they decided to accuse him and sought the help of Lachman Singh, who agreed to intervene as he himself had an interest in the land.

He made a dramatic appearance near the dead body. His pathos-laden cries put the sons to shame—Hai, chacha![1]

---

1. Father's brother.

You were a king! You deserved to die in state at home, not like this in an open field! You, who had everything!

Glaring at the sons he continued, Are you men or mice? How does it matter who killed him? The main thing is, he is dead. Hai, chacha! As long as you were alive, the lower castes never dared raise their heads. For fear of you, the sons of dushads and ganjus never dared attend government schools! Now who will take care of all these things?

Turning to the sons he said—Our duty now is to make sure that chacha receives all due honour by way of funeral rites. Take him home, inform the police—but don't name any names. The body is not to be taken to Tohri, not to be cut open for post mortems. Chacha died a hero's death. But the manner of his death is not what he deserved. People will talk. We must perform the ceremonies and burial with pomp and splendour. Dress up the body, place him on a big bed, and inform our entire Rajput clan.

Taking the sons aside he said—Forget your quarrels. My father is no more. Chacha's death is like the fall of Indra.[1] Invite all our clansmen. This is not the time to be divided. Makhan Singh, Daitari Singh, there are enough people to cause trouble if they see a chance.

Since Lachman Singh was busy with all this, Sanichari didn't find him home. She came away and sat with her head in her hands. Then she told Bikhni, 'Come, let's go see Dulan. He's a crafty old rogue, but he has a sharp mind. He's sure to show us a way.

After hearing them out, Dulan said, As long as there's a way of earning, why should anyone die of starvation?

What kind of earning?

Budhua's mother! Do readymade ways of earning exist? They may exist for malik-mahajans, but do they exist for dushads and ganjus? We have to make our own opportunities. How much money did your friend bring with her?

Twenty rupees.

Tw-en-ty whole rupees!

Yes. We've spent eighteen rupees on food.

If it was me, I'd have seen Mahabirji in my

---

1. Indra, one of the divine trinity of Brahma, Indra, and Shiva.

dreams long before the money ran out.

What on earth are you talking about, Latua's father?

Why? Can't you follow me?

No, what do you mean?

Before my money ran out I would pick up a nice stone from the banks of Kuruda river. I'd anoint it with oil and sindoor and proclaim that Mahabirji had come to me in my dreams.

But I don't even dream!

Arre, once you find Mahabirji you'll have no shortage of dreams.

Hai baba!

Everyone knows you. It won't work if you try it. But your friend is new here, we'd all believe her. Then you could present yourself and Mahabirji at the Tohri marketplace. Collect offerings from the devout.

Hanky-panky with a god? As it is Mahabirji's monkey followers don't leave any fruit on my trees!

It's trickery if you consider it trickery. Not otherwise. You have a sinner's mind, so you think it's trickery.

How's that? Eh, Latua's father?

Because . . . let me explain.

Go ahead.

Lachman's mother has rheumatism, doesn't she?

Yes, she does.

Well, she gave me ten rupees to bring her some holy oil from Chas. I didn't even go to Chas, just took her some oil from home after a few days. And it wasn't trickery, because I didn't consider it to be. She massaged herself with the oil yesterday, and today she walked on her own two feet to the fields to shit. You know what they say—If your mind is pure, the Ganga flows even through wood. Look here, Budhua's ma, there's no bigger god than one's belly. For the belly's sake everything is permissible. Ramji Maharaj said so.

Dulan's wife spoke up, Even when the old man lifts a pumpkin from the malik's field he claims it's on Ramji Maharaj's advice!

Bikhni said, We're in trouble. How can you help?

Give us old women some advice.

Bhairab Singh of Barohi village has just died.

Yes. His son killed him.

So what? In rich families the son kills the mother, the mother the son. Forget about who killed him. Amongst us, when someone dies, we all mourn. Amongst the rich, family members are too busy trying to find the keys to the safe. They forget all about tears. Our malik has ordered a fancy funeral. The funeral procession will be tomorrow afternoon. They need rudalis to wail over the corpse. They've got hold of two whores. In the households of the masters, whores weep for the dead. These two were probably Bhairab Singh's whores at one time, now they're wizened crows. They'll be no good. The two of you go, wail, cry, accompany the corpse. You'll get money, rice. On the day of the kriya ceremony you'll get clothes and food.

Sanichari felt an earthquake within. She exploded. Cry? Me? Don't you know? I can't shed tears? These two eyes of mine are scorched?

Dulan spoke in a cold, expressionless tone. Budhua's ma, I'm not asking you to shed the tears you couldn't shed for Budhua. These tears are your livelihood—you'll see, just as you cut wheat and plough land, you'll be able to shed these tears.

But will they take us?

What am I here for? If they don't get good rudalis, Bhairab's honour will suffer. The malik-mahajan demands honour even when he's a corpse. Bhairab's father and his generation kept whores too, but they looked after them. When they died, the whores mourned for them out of genuine affection and gratitude. But the Bhairab, Daitari, Makhan, Lachman Singhs of this world treat their labourers and whores alike—they tread them into the mud. So the randis don't make convincing rudalis. What vicious bastards that lot are! The worst is Gambhir Singh. He kept a whore, had a daughter by her. As long as the whore was alive, he kept the child in comfort. When the mother died, he told the girl, a whore's daughter is a whore—practise your profession and support yourself.

Chhi, chhi!

That girl is now rotting in Tohri, in the randi

bazaar. From a five-rupee whore she's down to a five-paise whore. Budhua's wife is there too. She's in the same state.

Who wants to hear about her?

Dulan said, Wear black clothing.

That's what we wear in any case.

Dulan took them along. On the way Bikhni said, If this kind of work comes along from time to time, and if we find jobs working the malik's fields or breaking stones, we'll be able to get along.

Sanichari said, Won't there be talk in the village?

So let them talk!

Bhairab Singh's accounts keeper Bachhanlal knew Dulan. Lachman had put him in charge of all the funeral arrangements, and it was no easy job. At the moment he was preoccupied with how he could pass off two shovels, a clothes rack and some brass utensils he needed for his own home as part of the funeral requirements. As soon as he saw the two women he said, You'll get three rupees each.

Dulan said, Such an important person is dead, and the rate for mourning him is only three rupees? At least five per head, huzoor.

Why?

They'll do such a good job, you'll want to give them a tip. Lachman Singh has ordered that ten, twenty, whatever it takes, he wants good rudalis. Two hundred rupees have been budgeted for this.

Bachhanlal sighed, wondering how Dulan knew so much.

Okay, five rupees each. Go, sit outside.

And they're to get rice as well.

They'll get wheat.

Give them rice, huzoor.

Okay.

And feed them well—they can't mourn convincingly on an empty stomach.

Dulan! How many bastards died to give birth to you? Go, wait outside. They'll get fed.

Bhairab Singh's senior wife ordered that the rudalis should be served generously with a snack of chivda and gur. Prashad's father hadn't left them lacking in anything.

As she filled her stomach on chivda and gur,

Sanichari thought that perhaps her tears had been reserved
for the time when she would have to feed herself by selling
them.

At first the randis paid no attention to the two old
village women. But Sanichari and Bikhni wailed so loudly,
and sang such well-chosen phrases in praise of Bhairab
Singh, that the marketplace randis had to admit defeat.
Sanichari and Bikhni wailed all the way to the cremation
ground and all the way back. Each of them earned five rupees
and two and a half sers[1] of rice. Bachhan told them, you must
come back for the kriya ceremony.

We'll definitely come, huzoor.

At the kriya they got clothes and feasted on puri,
kachauri and besan laddus.[2] They packed their portion to take
home. Sanichari shared some with Dulan's wife. Dulan
listened to all their news. He cursed, That bastard Bachhan
was allotted two hundred rupees for this job, and he got away
with spending only twenty.

That kind of thing is bound to happen, Latua's
father.

Tell your friend to keep her ears open on her
trips to the market. All the shops belong to the
landlords and moneylenders. Tell her to find out who's
ill, who's dying . . . otherwise we won't get
information in time. And she should tell them that
she can arrange for more rudalis.

How?

Go to Tohri. The randi bazaar.

My god!

Will your friend go?

Bikhni said, Yes, I'll go.

Dulan said, Do you think we always had so many
whores? It's these Rajput malik-mahajans who have created so
many randis.

His wife said, The whores have always been here.

No, they haven't. Not here. All the evil things
have been brought in by *them*.

They've also been here forever.

No. Earlier, when the area was under the raja

---

1. Unit of weight.
2. A kind of sweetmeat.

of Chhotanagpur, it was mostly jungle and hilly land,
and adivasis[1] lived here. This was a long, long time
ago. The Kols in the district town talk about it.[2]

The tale Dulan told them was very significant; it
explained clearly how the ruthless Rajputs infiltrated this
remote area of tribals, and from zamindars gradually built
themselves up to the status of jotedar/moneylenders and
established themselves as the masters of the area. The Rajputs
were warriors in the army of the raja of Chhotanagpur. About
two hundred years ago, in protest against the cruel oppression
practised against them, the Kol tribals revolted. The raja
immediately sent his army to put down the uprising. Even
after the rebellion was suppressed, the Rajput warriors'
aggression was not sated. They went on a rampage, killing
innocent tribals and burning down villages. So Harda and
Donka Munda started sharpening their arrows, and a fresh
tribal uprising was imminent. Then the raja sent his Rajput
sardars into the sparsely populated Tahad region. He told
them, take as much land as is covered by throwing your
swords in the air. Start at sunrise, and carry on till sundown.
There are seven of you, claim as much land as you can in this
way, then live off it.

That's how the Rajputs settled in Tahad, and how they
come to be masters of this region. From century to century
their holdings and power increased. Even now they take
possession of land, not by throwing swords in the air but by
shooting bullets at people and flinging flaming torches at
settlements. Once they were all related, and though the blood
ties have thinned, they all claim the same status and honour.

The lower castes live in settlements of decrepit mud
huts roofed with battered earthen tiles. The tribal settlements
look equally poor. In the midst of these are the towering
mansions of the maliks. There may be litigations and illwill
between the maliks, but they have certain things in common.
Except for salt, kerosene and postcards, they don't need to buy
anything. They have elephants, horses, livestock, illegitimate
children, kept women, venereal disease and a philosophy that
he who owns the gun owns the land. They all worship
household deities, who repay them amply—after all, in the

---

1. Aboriginal peoples.
2. Kol is the name of a tribe.

name of the deities they hold acres, which are exempt from taxes and reforms. Of course, there are differences between them—Daitari Singh has six toes, Banwari Singh's wife carries the blood of a lowcaste gwala[1] in her veins, Nathuni Singh has a stuffed tiger in his house.

After reminding them of all this he told them—These people need rudalis to prop up their honour. Now I've shown you the way, fight on.

Sanichari and Bikhni nodded. For them, nothing has ever come easy. Just the daily struggle for a little maize gruel and salt is exhausting. Through motherhood and widowhood they're tied to the moneylender. While those people spend huge sums of money on death ceremonies, just to gain prestige. Let some of that money come into Sanichari's home!

So Sanichari and Bikhni fought on. Everything in this life is a battle. Bikhni was not a woman of this village, but she became part of its life surprisingly easily. At sowing and harvest times she laboured in Lachman's fields; at other times, she visited the market and the shops near the bus-stop and brought home news—who was on his deathbed, who gasping his last in which malik's house. Then they would wash their lengths of black cloth. Put them on. Knot some churan into their anchals.[2]

Munching on the churan they'd hurry along to the big house. Sanichari negotiated with the malik's gomastha.[3] Their negotiation followed a fixed pattern.

The way we'll weep and wail, huzoor, we'll drown out even the chant of Ram's name! For five rupees and rice. On the day of the kriya ceremony we'll take cloth and food. Nothing more, nothing less. And if you need more rudalis, we'll arrange it.

The gomastha would agree to everything. What option did he have? Everyone wanted them after seeing their performance at Bhairab Singh's funeral. They were professional. The world belongs to the professional now, not to the amateur. The gomastha himself is professional at

---

1. Milkman—a low caste.
2. Churan is a spicy digestive preparation. Anchal is the end of the sari which is draped over the shoulders and the head.
3. Accounts keeper.

manipulating the fieldhands' accounts and increasing the
interest owed by peasant debtors. So professional is he, in fact,
that on a pittance of a salary, a mere ten rupees a month, he
manages to acquire his own fields, cattle, and even, if he so
desires, several wives. Professional mourning for the
unmourned dead is a regular business. In the big cities,
prosperous prostitutes competed for such jobs. In this region, it
is Sanichari who has taken up this business. After all, this is
not the big city. There are no prosperous prostitutes thronging
Tohri. So he has to agree to Sanichari's demands.

Just for wailing, one kind of rate.

Wailing and rolling on the ground, five rupees
one sikka.

Wailing, rolling on the ground and beating
one's head, five rupees two sikkas.

Wailing and beating one's breast, accompanying the corpse to the cremation ground, rolling
around on the ground there—for that the charge is six
rupees.

At the kriya ceremony, we want cloth,
preferably a length of plain black cloth.

This is the rate. Over and above this, you people
are like kings, can't you spare some dal,[1] salt and oil
with the rice? You've got the goddess Lakshmi captive at
home, you won't miss it! And Sanichari will sing your
praises everywhere she goes.

Business prospered. There was such a demand for the
pair who wailed at Bhairab Singh's funeral, that it was
almost like a war of prestige. Soon not just the landlords and
moneylenders, but lalas and sahus[2] began to ask for
Sanichari. In fact, when Gokul lala's father died he said,
Come every day till the kriya ceremony, Sanichari.

Gokul gave them sattu and gur every day, saying, We
acquire virtue by feeding you.

He also gave them good quality cloth, unlike the
malik-mahajans who palmed off the cheapest cloth. Sanichari
and Bikhni sold it in the market.

When he heard about the treatment they received at

---

1. Lentils.
2. These terms of reference indicate merchants and traders, who are just
below the malik-mahajans in social status.

Gokul's house, Dulan said, Good. From now on, you must keep visiting your clients' homes every day right till the kriya ceremony. They're bound to give something to rudalis. At such times no one really keeps a strict eye on expenditure.

Yes, they'll surely give something.

Sanichari exhaled tobacco smoke in sharp contempt. She said, These people can't summon up tears even at the death of their own brothers and fathers, won't they count their kriya costs? Do you know that Gangadhar Singh, a rich man like him, was stingy enough to use dalda instead of pure ghee on the funeral pyre of his uncle?

If they could cry for their own, where would you be?

They could shed a tear, at least!

Anyway. Let's talk of something useful.

Go ahead.

Rich people's goings-on. Nathuni Singh's mother is on her deathbed. His house is quite far away. He's said that he wants to hire you.

She's dying, not dead yet.

Arre, if you hear Nathuni's story you'll realize what sinners these people are. Nathuni Singh's land and wealth is all from his mother. Do you know who she is?

No. No one keeps close track of everyone's affairs the way you do.

She was the only child of Parakram Singh. The kinds of oppression that man practised! When I was a child, I remember how he punished one of his tenants, Hathiram Mahato. He tied the old man to a horse and set the horse galloping.

Yes, I heard about that.

Parakram's daughter inherited all his wealth. Nathuni owes everything to her. For some time she's been suffering from wasting fever and coughing up fresh blood. Apparently this disease is highly contagious.

No, no, Budhua had the same thing.

Budhua was a good man. Nathuni's ma is definitely evil.

Whatever. What were you saying?

Nathuni is such a worthy son that he's isolated

her in a single room at the far end of the compound. Aside from tying a goat to her bed, he hasn't bothered with any treatment. No hakim, no kabiraj, no doctor.[1] No herbal remedies, no medicines, no injections. She's still alive. Meanwhile, he's stocking up on sandalwood and sal wood for a sensational funeral pyre. Bales of cloth are arriving, for distribution at the kriya ceremony. He's preparing to feed brahmins and purchasing loads of ghee, sugar, dal, flour. He's buying utensils as well, to give the brahmins.

My god, and his mother's not even dead yet!

His mother's left to lie in her own excrement all day. Once every evening Moti the dushad woman cleans her up—no one's concerned about loss of caste or defilement any longer, it seems. They've kept a maid to sleep beside her at night. He's not willing to spend a paisa on trying to cure her, but plans to spend thirty thousand on her funeral!

You don't say!

He's shouting it to the rooftops. That's why I say their whole attitude is topsy-turvy. They don't care about the living, but once they're dead they hold grand funerals and try to raise their prestige. In this cold weather, he's taken away her warm quilt and given her a thin covering instead. He wants her to die quickly. You must visit their house every day till the kriya ceremony.

And what if they don't give us anything?

Don't worry, they will. Nathuni won't want to be outdone by Gokul lala. It'll be a loss of face before his community.

There's a saying that even the tiger shivers in the bitterly cold month of Magh. The cold soon kills off the old lady. Sanichari presents herself every day till the kriya. Nathuni has three wives. The eldest reluctantly doles out atta[2] and gur, grumbling. After all, she died of old age. Why spend so much on her kriya?

Nathuni's middle wife is the daughter of an

---

1. Hakim, kabiraj are practitioners of different schools of traditional medicine; 'doctor' refers to a practitioner of allopathic medical science.
2. Wheatflour.

extremely rich jotedar. Nathuni himself was rich because his father married the only daughter of a rich man—he wanted to do the same. It's bad luck that neither the eldest nor the youngest, but only the middle wife is treated as the beloved. She looks down on her marital home as poor compared to her father's, and resents her co-wives, because they are mothers of sons, whereas her child is a daughter, which lowers her status in the eyes of others. Overhearing the eldest wife she sneers, What's thirty thousand rupees for a kriya ceremony— less than nothing. May my father live long—but when he dies, then I'll show everyone how a kriya should be held!

The eldest co-wife replies sharply, Of course you will! After all, you have to cover up the fact that your father's sister has the blood of a lowly barber in her veins.

Don't make me laugh! My aunt and barber's blood! Everyone knows my aunt's husband in Gaya. But what about your widowed sister who lives with her dead husband's brother? How come you don't mention her?

This causes a major fight. But the middle wife must be truly virtuous. Her words were heard by the gods, and soon after her father was stricken by smallpox. She sent for Sanichari. She said, It must be true that those who die on an inauspicious Tuesday tug at the living. Otherwise why would my father get smallpox so soon after my mother-in-law's death? Here, Sanichari, here's a rupee tip.

Smallpox?

Yes.

Sanichari puts on an innocent air and asks—But I heard that the upper castes never got smallpox? That it was a disease of the poor and lower castes? That's why we take the government vaccination as well as appease the gods.

The government vaccine is like cow's blood.

Saying this, Nathuni's middle wife changed the topic. She said, You were there, weren't you, when the eldest wife and I quarrelled? With my father gone, I have no one. Here I'm surrounded by enemies. The others are given respect because they have sons. I'm the mother of a mere girl.

They respect you as well.

That respect is not for me, it's for my father Mohar Singh's wealth. My father didn't want to send me far away, that's why he arranged my marriage in a household where there are co-wives. Otherwise, as

Chauhan Rajputs, would we ever have married into such a family?

It's all a question of fate.

That's true. Listen, I'm off to my father's place. You and Bikhni will be required, plus another twenty randis. They'll get a hundred rupees plus rice. You two will get fifty rupees plus rice. You'll stay there till the kriya ceremony, you'll get your meals, and return after you've got the cloth from the kriya ceremony.

Huzoorain, your father's not dead yet.

The rot has set in. He has such a fit physique, fed on milk and ghee, the soul is reluctant to leave his body. When my mother-in-law died, you were given coarse rice and khesari dal.

And oil, salt, chillies.

Don't I know what they gave you? I know exactly how generous my eldest co-wife is! I'll give you rice, dal, oil, salt, potatoes and gur.

Huzoorain is a great benefactor of the poor!

And listen, you must really do a good job of the wailing.

Certainly—and shall we roll on the ground as well?

Yes, roll on the ground.

We'll roll on the ground, and shall we beat our heads too?

Yes, beat your heads.

Our foreheads will split.

Five rupees each extra for the two of you? Money's no problem, Sanichari. My father's cremation and kriya will be the stuff legends are made of. Everyone will talk about it. I want my husband and co-wives to burn with jealousy. I'm my father's only child. The lavishness should match what my father is bequeathing me. He drank his milk from a silver glass every day, had whores when he was a young man, kept them till he grew old, wouldn't touch anything but foreign liquor. He refused to remarry in case his second wife didn't treat me well.

Please give me some money, I'll have to pay the marketplace randis in advance. They're regular rascals.

Here, take.

The whole situation was quite complex. When someone died in a malik-mahajan household, the amount of money spent on the death ceremonies immediately raised the prestige of the family. The status of the rudalis also rose. The price for this was paid by the dushads, dhobis, ganjus and kols, from the hides of whom the overlords extracted the sums they had overspent. Mohar Singh's lavish death ceremonies became much talked about, with the lion's share of the profit going to the brahmins. Nathuni's middle wife never returned to her husband, and to prevent him laying his hands on her father's wealth, she began to spend lavishly on preparations for her daughter's wedding—this, however, took place after some years.

Sanichari reported her good fortune to Dulan. He smiled slyly and said, The coalminers have a union. Why don't you form a union of rudalis and randis? You can be the *pishiden.*[1]

Hai Ram!

Will you look for marketplace randis now?

What for?

Bikhni spoke up—I'll get them. It's the women who are ruined by the malik-mahajans who turn into whores.

Nonsense, they're a separate caste.

No, no, you know nothing about it.

Hordes of them gather at the Tohri marketplace.

Suddenly Dulan asked, Arre, Sanichari, remember Nawagarh's Gambhir Singh?

Baba! Don't I just! The one who used to roam about the Diwali mela on his elephant. He had a huge nose and a big goitre on his neck.

He's done something terrible.

What now?

Motiya was his kept woman. He maintained her like a wife. As for Motiya's daughter Gulbadan—he dressed her in silver anklets and let her play on his lap. He had vowed to marry her off respectably after Motiya died. Today I saw Gulbadan walking towards Tohri, her eyes red with tears. She was saying, they know how to produce children, but not how to look after

---

1. President.

their offspring. He's thrown me out. I asked, Why? She said, I merely complained to him that his neph_w was pestering me, and he glared at me and said—Your mother's been dead three months, and you're still hanging around here! Listen to my nephew's offer, or get out. You're the daughter of a whore, after all.

What a swine he is!

Dulan cleared his throat. He said, I felt terrible. Gulbadan said, How could he tell his own daughter to sleep with his nephew? And when I have a child by him? One day they'll kick that child out in the same way. It's better for me to work in the marketplace.

Sanichari heaved a sigh—With that face, she'll get snapped up by some rich merchant.

Bikhni said shrewdly—She's learned from her mother's fate, she won't let herself be tied to one man.

Bikhni went to Tohri and returned saying—My goodness! At the chance of earning money, a whole crowd of whores gathered around!

Got a good look at them?

That I did.

What're they like?

Cheap whores, selling themselves for a few annas, all old now. It's a hard life. They still have to stand around, eyes lined with kohl and lamps in their hands. They'll come as soon as they get to know that the old man's dead. One good thing!

What?

I saw your Budhua's wife, your son's wife.

In Tohri?

Yes. She looks older than you.

Don't talk about her.

She herself came up to me. She's been there ten years. Asked about her son.

What did you say?

What should I say? Why should I say anything? I didn't talk to her.

Good.

As she ate her vegetables and roti Sanichari thought of her daughter-in-law—of her huge appetite. When did she leave? It was the year the elephants overturned that railway engine. The year Budhua died. The mango tree was just a sapling then, now it bears fruit. Ten years at Tohri. Good thing Haroa ran away. At least he didn't find out about his mother.

After eating, the two of them took tobacco. Sanichari said—It was her fate. I wouldn't have turned her out after Budhua's death.

No, no, of course you wouldn't have.

Did she look very poor?

Very.

Sanichari fell silent.

Then Mohar Singh died.

The kriya was held with much pomp and splendour. Afterwards, when the old whores took leave, they addressed Sanichari and Bikhni respectfully, Huzoorain, if you need us again, just send word, we'll come.

Sanichari and Bikhni got a brass bowl and bamboo umbrella as well as cloth. Bikhni sold them in the marketplace and with the money bought a sackful of worm-eaten corn. She said, We can grind it into wheat or make porridge.

As time goes by, they settle into a rhythm. When someone dies, they work as rudalis. The rest of the time they survive on half-empty stomachs. And when there's nothing available? No problem. There aren't more than a couple of deaths a year. For the rest, just like everyone else, they labour in the fields or work for the malik, clearing land, or gather roots in the forest to feed themselves.

Bikhni surprised everyone. She didn't go to visit her son even once. She grew chillies in Sanichari's courtyard and sold them, then said, we should try growing garlic. Garlic sells well.

Gradually their reputation grew. Everyone wanted them as rudalis—sure, they weren't cheap, but they really did provide their money's worth, really did weep and wail and hit their heads in the dust. The praises these two sang in honour of the deceased made even their relatives think of them not as the died-in-the-bone devil's henchmen they were, but as divine beings born on earth to beguile them.

Things were going very well. In between two years were bad—Nathuni's eldest wife's brother was on his deathbed, but recovered after a stint in hospital. Lachman Singh's stepmother was virtually declared dead till a dangerous vaid came along and cured her.

Sanichari heaved a heavy sigh and said, Fate.

The village barber, Parashnath, was unhappy as well. He said—all this goes against dharma.

Why?

Look here, Budhua's ma. Earlier people fell sick, and in the natural course of things, they died. Along with births there should be deaths as well. Otherwise how will the world carry on? When the old become sick, they should die. All this business of old people being saved by doctors, vaids, hakims—I ask you, is it correct?

Sanichari sighed. Well, you're still better off than me. After all, you're in demand for births and marriages as well as deaths. No sooner is a wedding discussed than you're summoned! What will become of me!

Bikhni was not despairing. She said, Their time had not come, so they didn't die. No one lives beyond their fated time.

Dulan said, There's nothing to worry about. You're eating better than before, so you're worried about things going wrong. Don't you see the malik-mahajans' attitude? Lachman Singh's stepmother would weep at the sight of a good harvest because the money earned this year might not be repeated next year!

Sanichari said, Go on with you! Think you can turn everything into a joke?

After that Sanichari's luck improved. Bikhni returned one day, laughing—Great news!

What?

I'll have to sit down comfortably before I can tell you.

What's the news?

Getting irritated?

Get on with the news!

Gambhir Singh is dying.

Who told you?

Bikhni told her everything. She'd got the details straight from the barber, a reliable source. Does Sanichari remember that Nathuni's mother had the wasting fever and cough?

Yes, yes, of course I remember. Go on, Bikhni.

The way Nathuni treated his mother is now the norm in their community. This disease is considered beyond Shiva's skill. Any treatment or medication is seen as a grave insult to the god. Gambhir Singh has no close kin. His nephew is his heir. The nephew has isolated him in a shack in the yard, left him there with a black goat. At the sight of the goat Gambhir Singh said, this means I'm going to die. He gave instructions to arrange such a kriya for himself that it would leave everyone stunned. Everyone would realize that a great man had died.

Then? Go on, Bikhni!

Gambhir Singh is a really strange man! He's refusing medication, just does pujas and yagnas and havans all day long.[1] His wife insisted on calling a doctor. Even the doctor holds out no hope.

He isn't dead yet, is he?

He's bound to die! The nephew can't do a thing. The old man's summoned his lawyer and ordered that at least a lakh be spent on his kriya.

Why?

He's saying he's going to use up all his money. His nephew can take the proceeds from the land. He has no children, and he refuses to leave any money behind for his nephew.

So then?

Today or tomorrow, he's sure to die.

Meanwhile?

Meanwhile, I'll make a quick trip.

Where d'you want to go?

Ranchi.

Ranchi?! Why?

I met my nephew-in-law at the marketplace. He asked me to come, his daughter's getting married.

Daughter's getting married?

Bikhni let out a sigh—He says that wretch, my son, will probably be there. You're bound to ask why, if I want to see him, I don't just visit him at his in-laws. But that I can't do. However, if I do come across him on a visit to my nephew, no one can say anything. Even he won't realize that it's him

---

1. Different religious rituals.

I've gone to see.

Sanichari said, Well, since you put it like that I won't say anything. You say you want to see your son. But will you come back soon? Or will you stay on there?

How can I? That day I had walked out of my home, and I met you by chance. If you hadn't been there that day, what would I have done?

Don't forget about Gambhir Singh.

Oh, I'll be back within four days.

It was a three mile walk to the bus stop. Sanichari accompanied Bikhni, saw her onto the bus, advised her—It's eight rupees for a seat, squat in the aisle, you'll only have to pay two rupees.

Walking back, she mused on the exciting events taking place—to think of her friend, who knew nothing but foot paths, actually riding a bus, and going all the way to Ranchi! All that way to attend a relative's wedding! One's relatives live around one—not in far-off big cities like Ranchi!

Sanichari strolled home, chatting to people on the way. Everyone said—She's led such a hard, sad life. But finding Bikhni has been a blessing. What a hardworking old woman! The whole look of Sanichari's home has changed! This is what they call the game of chance—People who come from far away, strangers, can become as close as one's own kin. Like the bark of one tree grafted on to another.

At home, Sanichari felt restless. Out of habit she went into the forest to collect firewood, and returned with a bundle of dried twigs. Bikhni would never return emptyhanded. She'd bring back something or the other—either a couple of withered twigs or a length of rope she found on the path, or a pat of cowdung. Her most recent scheme was to rear a calf. Sanichari can't understand how, even this age, she's so interested in domestic and household matters.

A few days passed in this manner. Gambhir Singh's condition worsened as expected. Sanichari went there one day and discussed everything with the gomastha. In the process she learned that although it was being said that he had tuberculosis, actually he was dying of another disease. The excesses he had committed with untold women had given him venereal disease, which was rotting his flesh. That was why he was holding so many pujas and prayers, refusing medicine, courting death.

The accounts keeper said, He's decided to die during the period of the waxing moon.

Sanichari asked—Why? She thinks, Can the all-powerful malik-mahajans, who can do whatever they want, die when they want as well?

Who knows? replied the accounts-keeper with philosophic detachment—If you die during the period of the waxing moon, your soul goes straight to heaven, otherwise, like Yudhistira, you have to visit hell first.

Sanichari is not too familiar with puranic characters, but has no doubt of their greatness. Through calendar art the images of the epic and divine characters merge with the film actors who play their roles in movies. Trilok Kapoor and Yudhisthira, Abhi Bhattacharya and Sri Krishna and so on so forth.[1] Astounded she asks—What? Is the malik-mahajan Yudhistira?

The accountant explains patiently to this illiterate woman—Whatever the malik-mahajans say, happens. Right or wrong is a question of one's point of view. Now, wicked people might say that the malik had committed dacoity when his father was alive, in the time of the British, that he murdered hundreds of citizens of independent India, that he stole Lachman Singh's father's horse, that he burned down many dushad settlements with his own hands, that he ruined hundreds of young girls, that he's a big sinner. But the malik doesn't see it that way. So he's gathered astrologers and pandits[2] to determine what sin it could be that had caused him to be inflicted with this terrible disease.

Have they found out?

Found out what?

What the sin was?

Of course. When he was a boy he once hit a pregnant cow with a stick and killed it. This is his only sin.

Still she asks, will he really die in the period of the waxing moon as he wants to?

---

1. Trilok Kapoor and Abhi Bhattacharya are well-known matinee idols; Yudhistira is a mythological hero from the epic Mahabharata, and Sri Krishna the popular god.
2. Learned men.

Most definitely. Haven't you seen, till now, that whatever he wants, he gets? And I'll say this, he's done the right thing—if the money gets into his nephew's hands, it won't last.

Why?

All the malik's women have been Hindu, even the untouchables. But the nephew's randi is a mussalman.

Hai Ram!

Be prepared. I've worked here for so long. But after the kriya I won't stick on here. When the kriya is over, I'll leave. Malik has instructed that his kriya should be so grand that everyone forgets about Mohar Singh's funeral.

We'll go all out, huzoor.

Sanichari came away.

She returned home worried. Six days have passed. What's the matter with Bikhni? They live in an isolated village, not much communication with the outside, no one takes the bus anywhere. Who can possibly carry news of Bikhni from Ranchi? She sighed, and put some quilts out in the sun. Ground a little corn. Then she went to do her obligatory share of repair work on the panchayat meeting place. If not seen to regularly these mud huts got eaten away by termites. She returned home carrying a load of twigs on her head, straightened up and saw the stranger.

Unfamiliar man. Shaven head, bare feet.

Is Bikhni dead?

In a trice she understood everything. She asked—Are you her nephew-in-law?

Yes.

She felt a landslide within. But many deaths, deceptions, injustices, had hardened her endurance and self-control. She asked the stranger to sit down. She herself sat down, sat quietly for a while, then asked—How many days ago?

Four days.

Sanichari counted backwards and said—The day I went to Gambhir Singh's. What happened?

Asthma, complicated by a chest cold.

Something that started here or there?

She drank a glass of sherbet on the way.

Then?

She recalled how Bikhni could never resist colourful sherbets, digestive tablets, and candied fruit.

Then the wheezing became worse. My brother-in-law works in a hospital, he called a doctor, we started medicines and injections.

I never did that.

She would catch a few cockroaches, boil them and give Bikhni the water to drink. The wheezing would improve immediately.

Did she get to meet her son?

He didn't come. I'll be going to his place next, to give him the news. Did my aunt leave any belongings here?

No, nothing. You call her aunt, and she died in your house but all these days we didn't even know she had a family of her own, she was roaming the countryside alone, homeless . . .

I didn't know, or I'd have fetched her before.

You'd better be off. You have a bus to catch, it's a long way from here.

He left. Sanichari sat by herself and tried to comprehend the situation. What did she feel? Grief? No, not grief, fear. Her husband had died, her son had died, her grandson had left, her daughter-in-law had run away—there had always been grief in her life. But she never felt this devouring fear before. Bikhni's death affected her livelihood, her profession, that's why she's experiencing this fear. And why, after all? Because she's old. Amongst them, one works, if one can, till one's last breath. Ageing means growing old. Growing old means not being able to work. And that means death. Sanichari's aunt had lived till such an old age that they carried her in and out of the house like a bundle. In winter, they left her outside while they all went off to work, and came home to find her as stiff as wood, dead.

Sanichari didn't want to die like that. And why should she die? Her husband died, her son died, she didn't die of grief. No one does. After the worst disasters people gradually bathe, eat, chase away the goat nibbling the chillies in the yard. People can do anything—but if they can't eat, they die. If Sanichari has survived so much grief, she'll survive the loss of Bikhni. She's devastated, but she won't cry.

Money, rice, new clothes—without getting these in return, tears are a useless luxury.

Sanichari went to see Dulan.

He grasped the gravity of the situation at once, said, Look, Budhua's ma. It's wrong to give up one's land, and your profession of funeral wailing is like your land, you mustn't give it up. Can't you see how amusing it all is? One by one they're dying, you're going to wail, they're taking the pomp and splendour of the mourning so seriously, making it a matter of honour, they're fighting over it. Take Gambhir Singh, for example, he could easily call in a doctor and get cured, but he's not interested. He's more attracted by all the hoo-haa of a fancy funeral.

It's their business, what they fight over, what brings them honour.

It's your business too.

How will it help me to know all this stuff?

When Budhua's father died, didn't you take over his work in the malik's field?

Of course I did.

In the same way you have to take over from Bikhni.

How so?

You have to go yourself. Dulan spoke forcefully, angrily—It's a question of survival. You must go yourself.

To Tohri?

Yes, to Tohri. You'll go there, you'll find the whores, fix them up. Otherwise between Gambhir Singh's nephew and the gomastha, they'll keep all the money.

I'll go.

You must.

But what if . . .

Your daughter-in-law's there, is that it?

You know?

Of course. But so what? Isn't she also a ruined whore like the others? Get her as well.

Her?

Definitely. She needs to eat and earn like everyone else. This business of getting whores to mourn is really amusing. The wealth of these malik-mahajans is unclean money. There's no limit to it. Let a few whores from the bazaar come to their funerals. It's the malik-mahajans who've turned them into whores, ruined them, then kicked them out, isn't that so?

Yes.

She's not too clear about how they've become whores. She recalls how hunger drove her daughter-in-law to leave home, how Gulbadan looked upon her father's nephew as her brother, though both her father and the nephew considered her nothing but a whore. It all seems very confusing to Sanichari, who ponders the matter but can't fix on any direction to her thoughts. What does Dulan have to say?

Don't weigh right and wrong so much, leave that kind of thing to the rich. They understand it better. We understand hunger.

That's true.

So then, go on.

Won't the village speak ill of me?

Dulan laughed bitterly—What one is forced to do to feed oneself is never considered wrong.

Sanichari understood what he was trying to say.

Gambhir Singh died on the seventeenth day. When he was breathing his last, the gomastha sent Sanichari a message. She sent word that she was on her way with some more rudalis.

She got into her black clothes and went to Tohri. She felt no embarrassment about asking directions to the redlight area. Considerations of the stomach are more important than anything else. She walked in calling, Rupa, Budhni, Shomri, Gangu, where are you? Come along, there's rudali work for you.

The known whores gathered one by one. Soon there was a crowd, from the five-rupee whores to the one sikka ones.[1]

Huzoorain, you?

Bikhni's dead, Sanichari smiled. Seeing a familiar face in the crowd she asked—Budhua's wife? You come too, bahu. Gulbadan, you come along as well. Gambhir Singh has died; by wailing for him and taking their money you'll be rubbing salt in their wounds. Don't hold back. Take whatever you can. Come, come. Five rupees a head, everyone will get

---

1. A sikka is quarter of a rupee.

rice, and cloth at the kriya ceremony.

There was an eager bustle among the whores. The young ones asked, And us?

All of you come. When you grow old you'll have to do this anyway, so while I'm around let me initiate you.

Everyone was enjoying themselves hugely. Gangu brought Sanichari a mora to sit on.[1] Rupa brought her a cup of tea, a bidi. There was an air of excitement. Then they all set off for Nawagarh.

Gambhir Singh's nephew, his gomastha, everyone was astonished at the sight. The gomastha hissed—Have you brought the entire redlight district with you? At least a hundred whores!

Sanichari said, Why not? Malik said, make a great noise, a big fuss, something people will talk about. Is that possible with a mere ten whores? Move, move, let us get on with our work. The malik belongs to us now.

Gambhir's corpse stank of rotting flesh. The randi rudalis surrounded his swollen corpse and started wailing, hitting their heads on the ground. The gomastha began to weep tears of sorrow. Nothing will be left! Cunning Sanichari! Hitting their heads meant they had to be paid double! He and the nephew were reduced to helpless onlookers. While hitting her head on the ground and wailing loudly, Gulbadan turned her dry eyes in the direction of the nephew, cast him a leering wink and grinned. Then, listening to Sanichari's cry, she rejoined the chorus.

Translated from the original Bengali.

---

1. An indigenous stool.

Rudali
Usha Ganguli

Scene 1

Sanichari's home. At stage right, Sanichari sits grinding wheat in the chakki.[1] The monotonous creak of the chakki is the only sound. At stage left, her ailing son, Budhua, is lying on a charpoy.[2] Haroa, Budhua's child, is stretched out on his stomach under the charpoy, absorbed in playing with a toy. Sanichari's old mother-in-law Somri is lying towards the back, wrapped in a tattered covering.

SOMRI. I want food. Give me a roti! Arre oh Sanichari, give me a roti,[3] won't you? (*Sanichari continues to grind the chakki.*) Have you gone deaf or what? (*Sanichari carries on grinding. Budhua coughs painfully, turns over.*) You daain,[4] are you going to starve me to death?

SANICHARI. Parbatia will do the cooking when she gets back.

---

1. A stone mill.
2. A string cot.
3. Homemade unleavened bread.
4. A witch who devours human beings.

SOMRI. When will she come?

SANICHARI. I don't know.

SOMRI. You have the atta,[1] why don't you make some rotis?

The chakki stops.

SANICHARI. Then who'll do the grinding? Wants rotis made from other people's atta! We can have rotis only after I get my payment in kind. (*The chakki resumes. Budhua coughs again.*) Budhua, Parbatia isn't back as yet. (*The chakki slows down.*)

BUDHUA. She'll come, why are you worried?

SANICHARI. I kept telling you, don't let her go to the market, don't let her go. Now she'll hang around there all day.

BUDHUA. What would she do sitting at home?

The chakki stops.

SANICHARI. Why, I stay at home, don't I? I grind wheat for others, make cowdung cakes, gather firewood from the jungle. Just say that she wouldn't be happy staying at home. (*The chakki starts up again.*)

SUDHUA. You know everything, amma. You know that she steals from the money she makes selling vegetables, and buys all sorts of rubbish to eat.

SANICHARI. Don't I give her enough to eat?

BUDHUA. Her appetite is huge, amma.

Pause. The chakki continues.

SOMRI. That whore will never return, and I'll never get my rotis.

Sanichari turns around to glare at the old woman, then resumes her grinding with renewed energy.

BUDHUA. Amma, Parbatia was saying that she wanted to go work for Lachman Singh.

The chakki stops.

---

1. Wheat flour.

SANICHARI (*looking at Budhua*). Never.

BUDHUA. Why not?

SANICHARI. You're asking me why not? Once a young woman goes to work for Lachman Singh, the only place she's fit for is the whorehouse.

The chakki resumes. A little girl's voice is heard from outside.

CHILD (*off*). Chachi, oh chachi! May I have a few twigs of firewood? (*Sanichari doesn't respond, continues to grind the chakki.*) Amma needs some to light the fire.

SANICHARI (*angrily*). Last week your mother asked me to grind two and a half sers[1] of channa[2]. I got paid neither in cash nor kind—and now she wants firewood!

BUDHUA. Give it to her, amma.

SANICHARI. Go on, Haroa. Give her four sticks.

Haroa crawls out from under the charpoy and leaves to give her the firewood. Their voices are heard offstage.

CHILD. Give it to me! Give it to me!

BUDHUA. Dadia, look, she's snatching my toy!

SANICHARI. Get lost, you wretch! (*To Haroa*) Go, go to your father. (*Haroa returns and sits beside Budhua. The chakki resumes.*)

SOMRI. The bitch won't give me a thing to eat.

BUDHUA. Amma, why don't you give her something?

SANICHARI. What do I give her? Do I feed her from the huge pile of rotis your wife so graciously prepared before leaving?

SOMRI. You bitch, just watch out. Jackals will eat your dead body.

SANICHARI. Yes, I'm a bitch, a daain, my corpse will be eaten by jackals—is there anything else you wish to say?

SOMRI. Yes there is. Give me some roti.

---

1. A measure.
2. Gram, pulses.

The chakki stops.

SANICHARI. Hai Maiyya![1]

She rests her head on the chakki a moment, then gets up and starts grinding wheat from the second bag lying beside her. Budhua has a coughing fit. She quickly rises and hands him some water.

BUDHUA (*after drinking*). Oh god!

SANICHARI. If there was a god your illness would have been given to me instead.

BUDHUA. Why do you say such things, amma? As long as you're alive, my son has a chance . . .

SANICHARI. And I . . .

SOMRI. You'll kill off everyone else but you'll stay alive, you daain. As it is you've finished off your father-in-law, your brother-in-law, and your husband. Now you'll devour your son.

SANICHARI. Watch your mouth!

The chakki resumes.

SOMRI. Why shouldn't I say it? After all, you were born on an unlucky day, Saturday.[2] It's your destiny to devour everyone around you!

SANICHARI. And what great happiness did life bring you? You're Monday-born,[3] but you didn't get a better deal, did you? Arre, I've seen what lives they all live, those born on Tuesday, Wednesday, Thursday. As for you, you do nothing but bitch, bitch, bitch, all day long. Behaving as though your father left you a pile of wealth! Another word out of you and I'll throttle you.

Sanichari sits down and starts the chakki again. Her daughter-in-law enters. She notices her son sitting beside his father on the charpoy, grabs hold of him and dumps him angrily on the ground.

PARBATIA. Are you his father or his enemy?

SANICHARI. What's the problem?

---

1. An exclamation literally meaning 'Oh Mother!'
2. Sanichari' means one born on a Saturday or Sanichar.
3. Her name, Somri, means one born on Somvar, or Monday.

PARBATIA. Problem? He's got an infectious disease and he's sitting there with the child clasped to his bosom!

SANICHARI. If you're so concerned about the child, then why were you living it up in the market place all day? The entire household is hungry, no one's eaten.

PARBATIA. Am I under contract to feed the whole household? I went to the market to sell vegetables.

SANICHARI. To sell vegetables, or . . . Anyway, go on, give me the money. (*Parbatia hands her some money.*) What's this, only two rupees? You took a pile of brinjals and chillies to sell, and this is all you got for them? Or is there something more? Have a look, check—(*she moves towards the basket, but Parbatia snatches it up. They wrestle with it, and some things fall out: a colourful hair ornament, some bangles. Sanichari stares, aghast.*) Hai, hai, the whole household goes hungry, while her majesty preens and titivates! Where did you get these from, you bitch? Speak up!

PARBATIA. From the market, where else?

SANICHARI. Where did you get the money? Go on, tell me, you bitch, did you spend our vegetable money on this rubbish? (*Parbatia doesn't answer. Sanichari grabs her by the hair.*) Where did you get the money? Answer me! Who gave it to you?

BUDHUA. Let her go, amma!

PARBATIA (*freeing herself*). Don't you dare touch me! You can't even provide a few rotis for your family! And you think you can push me around, you bitch?

SANICHARI. I'll do it as often as I like! Her husband is lying there sick, and the whore preens in trashy trinkets!

PARBATIA. What's it got to do with you, oh mother of my husband? Huh! Husband indeed! Can't provide a square meal, but lays claim to being a husband.

SANICHARI. Look Parbatia, give me a straight answer. Who gave you all this?

PARBATIA. No one. I bought it out of my earnings. From the money I made splitting wood for Lachman Singh.

SANICHARI (*springing forward to hit her*). You swine, you bitch, you went to Lachman Singh! When I've warned you over and over again to stay away from that devil!

PARBATIA. He may be a devil, but at least he's a man! Not like this one, coughing his lungs out all day!

SANICHARI. Parbatia, you'll get a thrashing for that!

The two of them fight, grappling with each other. Dulan's wife, Dhatua's mother, enters.

DULAN'S WIFE. What's the matter, Sanichari? What's happened?

Parbatia snatches up her trinkets and stomps off stage in a rage.

SANICHARI. Nothing. It's my karma that's to blame (*she sits down at the chakki*).

DULAN'S WIFE. Have you finished the grinding?

Sanichari fills a bag with flour and hands it to her.

SANICHARI. Parbatia! Oh Parbatia! (*There's no reply.*) Haroa, please fetch the kneading dish from inside.

DULAN'S WIFE. Wait, I'll get it. (*She goes in, and returns with it. She uses it to remove a measure of flour from the bag and places it before Sanichari.*) Here, this is your share. How's Budhua?

SANICHARI. Not good.

DULAN'S WIFE. Have you given him any medicine?

SANICHARI (*showing her the two rupees*). Her highness came back with this. A measly two rupees. Do I spend it on medicine, or . . .

DULAN'S WIFE. Don't worry, Sanichari. I'm sure everything will work out all right. (*Handing over a sack*) Here, Bisesar's mother sent this. Have it ground by tomorrow morning. (*Gets up*) Okay, I'm off (*leaves*).

SANICHARI (*angrily*). Parbatia! Oh Parbatia!

PARBATIA (*off*). What is it?

SANICHARI. Enough of your tantrums. Come on out.

PARBATIA (*storms in and stands facing her*). What d'you want?

SANICHARI. Here, take this atta and make the rotis.

PARBATIA. I can't make the rotis.

SANICHARI. Why, you shameless hussy! Your child is starving, your husband is hungry, and you say you won't make rotis? Who'll make them, then? Your father? If you're living here, you'll have to do your share of work, understand?

PARBATIA. I'll do it today. But I'm telling you once and for all, I'm only staying here as long as he's alive. The moment he dies, I'm leaving—or I'm not my father's daughter.

She picks up the full kneading dish and stalks off. Sanichari looks after her, then casts a quick glance at Budhua. She resumes grinding the chakki with a vengeance. The light dims slowly.

Scene 2

Sanichari's home. Afternoon. Somri is lying in her usual place. Budhua is on the charpoy, covered with a sheet. He breaks into painful, hacking coughing fits, then lies down again. Meanwhile, with the help of a mirror propped up against the wooden handle of the chakki, Parbatia is busy arranging her hair. Her son sits beside her, fiddling with her trinkets and make-up things. She slaps his hand away, then, when he touches them again, yells at him.

PARBATIA. I told you not to touch, you bastard! Go on, get lost!

Haroa, chastened, goes to his grandmother. Somri consoles him and gathers him close.

SOMRI. Come, beta, come to me. (*Muttering*) Daain! (*Budhua is hacked by a particularly violent fit.*) Hey Parbatia! Parbatia! Can't you hear?

PARBATIA. What is it?

SOMRI. Get up and give Budhua some water to drink . . .

PARBATIA (*plaiting her hair*). What are you making such a fuss for? I'm just getting up.

Budhua's fit worsens.

SOMRI. Arre, you bitch, hurry up, can't you! The boy will die.

Give him some water.

PARBATIA (*completes her plait*). God! Bloody nuisance! (*She gets up, fills some water in a tumbler from the jar, then offers it to Budhua.*) Go on, drink. Let's get it over with. (*Continues to stand there, proffering the water*) What's the problem? How long d'you expect me to keep standing here? (*Budhua, hacked by coughs, extends his trembling hand for the tumbler, but knocks it out of her clasp. At the sound of the clatter, Somri immediately calls out.*)

SOMRI. What happened, Parbatia? What's the matter? (*Parbatia doesn't reply.*) Arre oh, you daain, will you tell me what's happened?

PARBATIA (*in a flustered tone*). N-nothing . . . the glass fell . . .

She continues to look searchingly at Budhua, then stands, thinking. She seems to come to a decision, picks up the fallen tumbler and goes in. She emerges with a cloth bundle which she places near the chakki. Somri is lying quiet, with the child beside her. Feverishly, Parbatia goes in once again, returns with some clothes and stuffs them into the bundle, then gets up, goes to the large storage pot and reaches for the pouch of money kept inside. All at once Sanichari's voice is heard off stage. Parbatia quickly shoves the pouch back in, snatches up a cloth, and begins to wipe up the spilled water. Sanichari enters carrying a bundle of twigs, and lowers it to the floor.

SANICHARI. What's the matter . . . couldn't you hear . . .

PARBATIA. Ask your son what the matter is.

Sanichari goes up to Budhua and turns him over. There is blood flowing from his mouth and his eyes are turned up. Seeing him in this terminal state Sanichari loses her calm.

SANICHARI. What's happened to you, beta? (*He utters broken sounds.*) Eh, Parbatia, run and fetch the vaidji.[1] This doesn't look good at all.

PARBATIA. Can't you see I'm busy? Besides, my head aches in this afternoon heat.

---

1. Traditional healer/doctor.

SANICHARI. My son is dying, Parbatia.

PARBATIA. What can I do about it? I can't go anywhere.

SANICHARI. Are you a human being or an animal? Is this how your father brought you up?

PARBATIA. My father taught me well. He taught me to stay far away from the dying.

SANICHARI (*furious*). You daain, how dare you? Come here and sit beside him. Don't move from here. I'll go fetch the vaidji.

Sanichari leaves. Parbatia gets up, looks closely at Budhua. A pause. She casts a quick glance at the still Somri, then darts in and brings out her bundle. She takes the money pouch out, puts it into her bundle, and begins to hurry out. She catches sight of her son and stops. A pause. Then she abruptly runs out.

SOMRI. Parbatia, hasn't Sanichari returned yet? Is Budhua sleeping?

The child awakes as well.

HAROA. Maai . . .

SOMRI. Looks as if your mother's gone to the market.

HAROA. Maai, who'll make the rotis?

SOMRI. Are you hungry, beta? Want to eat something? I have some pickle, do you want a little? Go, fetch a bit of atta in this bowl.

HAROA. Dadia will beat me.

SOMRI. No one will beat you. Go, fetch some.

Haroa fetches some atta in the small bowl. Sanichari enters with the vaidji.

VAIDJI. You people have no respect for time. Such impatience! Can't wait for even a minute. I was looking forward to my afternoon nap after a good meal, and you have to drag me here. Where's this son of yours?

SANICHARI (*going up to Budhua*). Budhua, oh Budhua, wake up. Look, vaidji's here.

The vaid approaches the charpoy, then stops. He frowns, places his hand under Budhua's nostrils.

VAID. Lower him to the ground and give me my fee.

SANICHARI. What's happened to him, vaidji? Why don't you examine him?

VAID. You've dragged me all the way here in the afternoon heat to examine a corpse!

SANICHARI. What are you saying, vaidji? My Budhua . . . check him carefully, vaidji.

VAID. What am I to check? He's as stiff as a log. Come on, hand over my money, let me go home and rest.

SANICHARI. He was still breathing when I left to call you. (*Pleads*) Just examine him once more, please . . .

VAID. What a nuisance this is! D'you think I'm lying? Feel him and see, he's cold all over.

SANICHARI. Budhua, oh Budhua.

VAID. He's not going to answer you. He's dead.

Hearing this, Somri breaks out into loud wails. A villager enters, takes in the situation and hurries out.

VAID. Hurry up and give me my money. It's getting late. And I'll have to cleanse myself in the river before going home. (*Sanichari fixes him with an angry glare.*) What're you glaring at me for? Take out the money and pay up.

SANICHARI. What kind of a man are you, vaidji? My son is lying dead and all you can think of is your fee.

VAID. Did you hear that? Did you hear what this daain said? She's dragged me here by force, and now she's thumbing her nose at me! Arre, till I get my money I'm not moving an inch! All you low caste people are the same—no knowledge of religion, no faith, no education!

Hearing the noise, Dulan enters with his wife and some other villagers.

DULAN. What's happened, Sanichari? Why all the commotion?

SANICHARI. Dulan . . . my Budhua . . .

DULAN'S WIFE. Hai Ram, what're you saying? Quick, lower

him to the ground. (*She begins to wail in mourning*) Budhua
re!

A VILLAGER. Arre bhaiya, he was all right this morning . . .

2ND VILLAGER. Why don't you examine him one more time,
vaidji?

Bijua enters on the run.

BIJUA. What's happened, bhaiya, what's happened?

VILLAGER. Arre bhaiya, Budhua's passed away.

BIJUA. Arre, how did this happen . . . smash the water pot,
brothers.[1] Come, brothers, let's lower the corpse to the
ground.

*Several villagers move forward to lend a hand, but the vaid stops
them.*

VAID. 'Stop! I forbid you to touch the body. First, my fee.

SANICHARI. Just wait and see—when you die your corpse will
be eaten by jackals. I'm giving you your precious money!

*She goes in. Some neighbouring women enter wailing. They sit down
by the dead body. The body is lowered to the ground. The child
comes and sits by it. Sanichari enters, stunned.*

DULAN'S WIFE. What's the matter, Sanichari?

SANICHARI. I can't find Parbatia . . .

VAID. It's all over now, just give me my money.

DULAN. We're just giving it, vaidji. (*He goes up to the stricken
Sanichari.*) Come, give the money . . .

SANICHARI. Dulan, I'm finished. Parbatia has taken
everything I had and run off.

DULAN. What're you saying?

DULAN'S WIFE. No, no, Sanichari, it must be here
somewhere.

SANICHARI. I'm sure she's run off . . .

VAID. Arre, now what's up?

---

1. A ritual in a household where there has been a death.

DULAN. But . . . what about Vaidji's money?

DULAN'S WIFE (*untying a fifty-paise coin from the corner of her sari*). Here, give him this and let's get rid of him.

DULAN (*handing the vaid the coin*). Vaidji, please accept this for now, we'll send you the rest later.

VAIDJI. Fifty paise? Do you take me for a beggar? I knew something like this would happen! You low caste people are all the same! Just you call me again and see . . . Daain that you are!

Vaidji leaves in a huff. The neighbouring women whisper between themselves, then begin to wail again.

WOMAN 1. Hai, Ram! To die at such a young age!

WOMAN 2. Hey, Sanichari, where's your daughter-in-law gone?

DULAN'S WIFE. She's gone to the market, where else?

WOMAN 3. Yes, I know exactly which market she's gone to!

WOMAN 2. Her husband's lying dead and she's gone to the market!

WOMAN 1. Parbatia's ways are hardly a secret in the village . . .

DHATUA'S WIFE. This isn't the time or place to talk like this, chachi.

WOMAN 2. Why should I keep quiet? Arre, she used to live it up all day with that hefty young brown-eyed fellow—you know the one I'm talking about, the bangle-seller—using the market as an excuse to be out of the house . . .

WOMAN 3. Gunni's father was saying that he treated her to halwa-puri[1] all day long . . .

WOMAN 2. Sanichari's luck is really bad.

WOMAN 1. She has a heart like a stone, the daain. Not a single tear has she shed . . .

DULAN'S WIFE. Will you all shut up with your chatter?

---

1. Delicacies usually associated with special occasions.

Dhatua's wife, come here. (*The girl goes to her.*) Take Haroa home, give him something to eat and drink, and put him to sleep. (*To Haroa*) Go, beta ....

The child leaves with Dhatua's wife. Bijua detaches himself from the cluster of waiting men and moves forward.

BIJUA. Bhauji, better make some arrangements, the corpse can't just lie here like this.

DHATUA. Once the sun goes down there'll be a problem, chachi.

DULAN. Don't worry about it, Sanichari, we'll manage everything. (*To Natua*) Hey Natua, listen here. Take Sankar and bring the firewood. (*To Bijua*) Now tell me, what else will we need?

BIJUA. Arre, there's lots to be done—do you think a kriya ceremony comes cheap? Mohanlal pandit's fee, chivda, dahi, gur[1]—and won't you need to sacrifice a goat?

A VILLAGER. All this . . . ?

BIJUA. What else? On the fourth day one has to feed five brahmins on dahi and gur. I tell you, living is tough for us poor people, but dying is even worse.

DULAN. Don't lose heart, Sanichari. One has to spend on such occasions, there's no way out. Is there anything you can sell?

SANICHARI. Whatever little bit I managed to put away, Parbatia's taken with her. I have nothing, Dulan, nothing.

DULAN. You can sell this chakki of yours.

SANICHARI. What are you saying, Dulan? If I sell this, how do I earn? What will I eat?

NATUA. I've arranged for the bamboo and firewood, Dulan chacha.

BIJUA. Now let's get moving, bhai.

Somri begins her ritual wailing. The other women join her.

DULAN'S WIFE. Cry, Sanichari, cry . . . it will make you feel better.

---

1. Chivda—parched rice; dahi—curd; gur—jaggery.

DULAN. Don't delay in sending the chakki off . . .

The women continue to wail. Sanichari slowly sits down by the chakki. The lights dim.

Scene 3

Sanichari's home, eight or nine years later. Morning. Haroa is now a youth. A cheap harmonica in his mouth, he blows away as he sits on the charpoy, tending his hair in front of a propped up mirror. Sanichari enters carrying a basket of grain.

SANICHARI. What's up, Haroa? Aren't you going to work?

HAROA. Don't feel like it today, Dadia.

SANICHARI. Why, beta, what's the matter? (*Haroa doesn't respond.*) Eh, Haroa, say something . . .

HAROA. My stomach's paining . . . (*He glances at her.*)

SANICHARI. Don't make excuses. Nowadays your heart isn't in your work . . arre oh, you lordling (*Haroa looks at her*) Come here, sit next to me (*he comes up to her*). Now tell me, what's bothering you?

HAROA. I just don't feel like doing my work, dadia.

SANICHARI. How I had to beg and plead to get you your job at Lachman Singh's, and now you say you don't feel like working . . . (*she keeps sorting the grain*).

HAROA. I work like a donkey all day long, carrying heavy loads . . . I hate it.

SANICHARI. Arre beta, if you don't work, how will you get money? (*Haroa is silent.*) Go, beta, your employer will get annoyed.

HAROA. I'll do some other work.

SANICHARI. Where will you find another job? Who'll give you one? Look, Haroa, I'm getting on, now. I can't work the way I did before. It's upto you now, beta . . . I'm relying on you. You're all I have, there's no one else to look out for me . . . You saw how Somri died, lying in her own filth, do you want me to end up like that . . . ?

HAROA. Lachman Singh's son thrashes me with his shoe.

SANICHARI. If you don't work properly, of course he'll beat you! You don't get money for nothing, you have to work for it.

HAROA. He makes me slave all day and pays me a measly twenty rupees a month. . .

SANICHARI. Plus a daily meal.

HAROA. Does that mean he can hit me when he likes, abuse me as he likes . . . ?

SANICHARI. That's a poor man's fate, beta—the kicks of his master. Go on, beta, go to work . . .

HAROA. Okay, I'll go, but dadia, I want a coloured vest from the market . . .

SANICHARI. Get your wages, and you'll get your vest. Now run along, you so-and-so.

Haroa gets up and prepares to leave for work. He combs his hair carefully before the mirror. Bijua the barber enters.

BIJUA (*on seeing Haroa*). So, young man, how are things? (*He sits beside Sanichari.*) Well, bhauji, how's everything?

SANICHARI. Can't you see? I'm living in the lap of luxury, gorging on halwa-puri! (*As she winnows dal*) What brings you here so early in the morning?

BIJUA. Why? Can't I drop in to see my bhauji just like that?

SANICHARI. You wicked old so-and-so, you still haven't changed your ways . . . go on, tell me why you've come.

BIJUA. I will, I will first let me relax a bit.

HAROA (*ready to leave*). Dadia, I'm hungry. Give me something to eat.

SANICHARI. Beta, there's nothing at the moment.

HAROA. But I'm hungry. How can I work on an empty stomach?

SANICHARI. There's nothing in the house . . . once I finish winnowing this dal I'll get some atta in return. Only then will I be able to cook—here (*untying some money from the corner of her sari*), take this twenty-five paise, pick up something on your way. (*Haroa's about to leave*) Wait a bit, beta! (*she gets up, goes to the urn, takes out a blessed charm and ties it on him*).

HAROA. What's this?

SANICHARI. I got it from Mohanlal specially for you.

HAROA. I don't want to wear it!

SANICHARI. Don't say that, beta, it's blessed by Shivji. Wear it, it'll be good for you. (*After tying it on him she strokes his head. His carefully combed locks are now displaced, so he combs his hair again, and prepares to leave.*) Listen, beta, there are lots of horned cattle in the marketplace. Be careful not to get too close to them.

HAROA. Okay.

SANICHARI. And listen, don't fall into bad company . . . all right?

HAROA. I've heard you.

SANICHARI. Don't touch cigarettes or bidis.[1]

HAROA. All right, all right!

Haroa leaves. Sanichari sits down once again and takes up the winnowing tray.

SANICHARI. Now out with it, old man. What is it?

BIJUA. Hold on, old woman. We have time enough for work. First let me give you some ripe gossip.

SANICHARI. What?

BIJUA. Last week, I went to Tohri—

SANICHARI. So what's new? Ever since your wife passed away, you've been a regular visitor there, you rascal you.

BIJUA. Will you listen? In the whores' quarter there I came across Parbatia.

SANICHARI. Why're you telling me this?

BIJUA. What can I say, Bhauji? She's looking older than you.

---

1. A cheap smoke.

At first I didn't recognize her—

SANICHARI. Listen, Bijua, don't talk about her to me. I don't want to hear a word about her.Whether she lives as a whore or as someone's wife, that's her business. Why are you concerned? Let's talk about something useful.

BIJUA. Yes, yes . . . I was just talking casually. Actually, Lachman Singh's nephew Ratan Singh is having his tilak ceremony. The house is full of relatives. They need a lot of dal and wheat ground. So the malik has summoned you.

SANICHARI. What will I make out of it? I don't want to grind mounds of stuff and get just a fistful of grain in return.

BIJUA. Arre no, bhauji. There's enough work for several days. The malik will pay you well.

SANICHARI. If that's true, then, old man, may you prosper!

BIJUA. And why not? Both of us will gain by it. (*They laugh.*)

SANICHARI. Haroa didn't tell me about this ceremony at Lachman Singh's . . .

BIJUA. You mean your grandson? How would he know?

SANICHARI. Why, he works in Lachman Singh's godown.

BIJUA. But I go there so often, I've never seen him there.

SANICHARI. What are you saying, Bijua? Doesn't Haroa go to Lachman Singh's?

BIJUA. Arre Bhauji, I've seen all Lachman Singh's employees, but I swear I've never once seen Haroa.

SANICHARI. Then where does he go when he says he's going to work?

BIJUA. He must be hanging around having a good time with the loafers in the market place, what else? (*Sanichari keeps silent, suppressing her anger.*) These are dangerous years, bhauji, when a boy is growing into a man. You should ride him on a light rein. (*He gets up*) Okay, I'm off, bhauji. Come across to Lachman Singh's this evening. If you earn some money, it will be a help.

Bijua leaves. Sanichari picks up the winnowing tray and begins to ply it with a vengeance.

Scene 4

Evening. A ray of the setting sun lights up Sanichari's house. Dhatua's wife is putting her child to sleep. Dulan's wife is standing with a sack in each hand. Sanichari is measuring flour into the sacks. Misri is counting.

MISRI. One, two, three, four, that makes one ser. One, two, three—what's this, one quarter less? I gave you a full two sers.

SANICHARI. Don't lie! How dare you claim you gave a full two sers—you gave me a quarter less!

MISRI. Hai Ram! First she steals, then she gets aggressive! She's swiped my dal and now she's acting innocent!

SANICHARI (*to Dulan's wife*). Did you hear that? Why did I take on any work for this she-devil!

MISRI. Hey, Sanichari, watch your mouth! Call me a she-devil and I'll cut off your tongue!

DULAN'S WIFE (*to Misri*). Why are you causing trouble? Take your dal and give her what's due to her.

MISRI. Why should I? She's already swiped a quarter of a ser, why should I give her anything extra?

SANICHARI. You're standing here in my house and calling me a thief! The whole village knows me for what I am! (*She thrusts the sack at her*) Take your sack and get out! If you set foot in here again I'll break your head!

MISRI. You'll break my head, will you? I'll gouge out your eyes and shove you in the well, daain that you are! (*She takes her sack and stamps out*).

DULAN'S WIFE. She makes everyone's life miserable.

DHATUA'S WIFE. And she didn't give you your share, chachi.

SANICHARI. I spit on her! Nowadays you can't count on anyone!

Dulan enters.

DULAN. What's the matter, Sanichari?

SANICHARI. Nothing. Come and sit, Dulan. (*She readies the*

charpoy for him.)

DULAN (*handing his wife a twist of paper*). Here, here's some ajwain.[1] Make it into a paste and give some to Dhatua . . .
Dulan's wife hands it to Dhatua's wife, who lifts up her child and leaves.

DHATUA'S WIFE. I'm going, chachi.

DULAN. What's the matter, Sanichari, you look very disturbed.

SANICHARI. It's nothing.

DULAN. Why isn't Haroa going to work nowadays?

SANICHARI. Bijua was telling me the same thing.

DULAN. I've seen him with my own eyes, roaming around with the fairground magicians.

DULAN'S WIFE. Hai Ram, they have a terrible reputation. I hope they haven't enticed him by putting a spell on him or something!

SANICHARI. Just let him come! I'll break his legs! And as for you, Dulan, when you saw him misbehaving why didn't you give him two tight slaps?

DULAN'S WIFE. He's grown up now, you can't just slap him around.

Natua Dushad enters.

NATUA. Ram Ram, Dulan chacha.

SANICHARI. How much did you sell?——

NATUA. The bhindi sold well,[2] but there're still some chillies left.

DULAN'S WIFE (*looking in the basket*). What d'you mean 'some'? There are lots of chillies left.

SANICHARI. Go, put it inside. (*Natua goes inside to leave the basket.*) This Natua Dushad never manages to sell well . . .

DULAN. Arre, he must be swiping half the money, I'm sure of it!

---

1. A digestive herb.
2. Bhindi—okra.

Natua returns.

NATUA (*to Sanichari*). Here you are, four rupees eighty paise.

SANICHARI. Only four rupees eighty paise?

NATUA. What else?

SANICHARI. Look, Natua, you really fool around with the accounts . . .

NATUA. Fool around? Look here, if you don't trust me, get someone else to sell your vegetables. I'm not interested.

DULAN. Hey, you bastard, I'm wise to your sly ways. Hand over the rest of the money!

NATUA. Look chachi, see what Dulan chacha's saying . . .

DULAN'S WIFE. Why are you two quarrelling?

SANICHARI. Okay, okay, here—take your two rupees, and come nice and early on market day.

NATUA. Yes, of course I'll come early. If it wasn't for me, all your vegetables would rot . . . and you call me a thief! (*He leaves.*)

SANICHARI. It's true. If it wasn't for Natua Dushad, all my vegetables would go waste. Budhua planted them with such love!

Haroa enters, playing his mouth organ. He stops when he sees the visitors. Sanichari turns to look at him.

SANICHARI. Well, Mr High-and-mighty, where were you all day?

HAROA. Why? I was working in the godown.

SANICHARI. How many sacks did you stack?

HAROA. Umm . . . about . . .

SANICHARI. One more lie and I'll pull your tongue off, you bastard!

HAROA. What's the matter?

SANICHARI. It's been ten days since you went to work, and you're asking me what the matter is?

HAROA. Which swine tattled on me? (*He glances at Dulan.*)

SANICHARI. I'm telling you that you haven't been going to work.

HAROA. Yes, I haven't been going. I refuse to do that kind of work. He pays a pittance, and on top of that he kicks me around! Who's going to work in a job like that?

SANICHARI. Arre, you son of a bitch, is Lachman Singh your kith and kin, that he's going to pay you for doing nothing?

HAROA. I won't go to Lachman Singh's.

SANICHARI. Yes, I know, you prefer to hang out with those no-good magicians.

HAROA. Yes, I do.

SANICHARI. You'd better listen to me, Haroa. If you don't go back to work tomorrow, I'll throw you out of the house.

HAROA. You won't have to—I'm leaving.

SANICHARI. Go, then! Get out right now!

HAROA. I'm going, I'm going! Can't provide a square meal, and orders me around!

SANICHARI. What did you say? I don't feed you well? My whole life has gone in feeding and raising you, and now you turn around and say I don't give you enough to eat?!

HAROA. No you don't. You never gave anyone enough to eat. You starved my grandmother, you drove out my mother, you killed off my father . . .

SANICHARI. Haroa . . .

In a fit of rage, she snatches his mouth organ out of his hand and flings it on the ground.

HAROA. Why did you throw away my mouth organ?

DULAN. Why are you talking to your grandmother like this, Haroa . . . .

HAROA. I'll speak as I want! Who are you to interfere, you old sneak? She's a dain, she's finished off all the others, now she'll devour me . . .

SANICHARI (*picking up a stick*). What did you say? I'm a daain?

You called me a daain? You too? You're no different from your mother! (*She beats him.*) Take that! and that! Calling me a daain!

Dulan and his wife try to separate the two, and prevent her from hitting him, saying 'Don't hit him, let him go.'

SANICHARI. No, today I won't let him get away with it (*continues to beat him*). Leave this house, get out of here!

HAROA (*choked and tearful*). I'm going! And I'll never come back! Can't provide for me, can't give me enough to eat! Why do you beat me? You've devoured everyone, you dain! I'll never come back! You'll have to stay here all alone.

SANICHARI. You get out right now, you swine!

Haroa takes his mouth organ and starts to walk out.

DULAN (*trying to stop him*). Hey, Haroa, don't go . . .

HAROA (*shoving him aside*). Out of my way, you stupid bastard!

He leaves. Sanichari is as if stunned.

DULAN. That was not right, Sanichari. He's a young man now. You shouldn't have hit him.

DULAN'S WIFE. You could have explained things nicely. Why did you have to hit him? Suppose he takes it to heart?

DULAN. It doesn't look good to me at all . . .

DULAN'S WIFE. Then what are you standing here for? Go after him, calm him down, bring him back. (*Dulan leaves.*) You didn't do the right thing, Sanichari. (*Sanichari remains silent*) Well . . . I must be off, my daughter-in-law's on her own. You'd better light your lamps . . .

She leaves. Sanichari remains standing, silent, for a while. She looks down at the stick in her hand, then flings it away. She starts to pick up the scattered grain from the floor. The light dims.

Scene 5

Evening. A group of men and women are seated·at the back, eating and drinking. Some children are running here and there, playing with carts. The hustle and bustle of a mela or fair. Seated on the stump of a tree,

Bikhni is eating a banana. She throws the skin on the ground, and takes another banana from her cloth bundle. A sweet-seller is on his way back from the mela.

BIKHNI. Hey, you, come here . . . let's see what you've got . . .

SWEET-SELLER. Do you want to buy or just look?

BIKHNI. First I'll look, then I'll buy. Show me . . .

He lowers his glass case to the ground. She picks out a sweet from it, and sniffs it.

SWEET-SELLER. Hey, old woman, what're you sniffing it for?

BIKHNI. Your mother may be an old woman, I'm not. Trying to pass off stale stuff and make a fool of me . . .

SWEET-SELLER (*laughs*). He, he, he, I made them just this morning and you're calling them stale!

BIKHNI. So, how much?

SWEET-SELLER. Four for a rupee.

BIKHNI. What a crook! Just four! If you give me six for a rupee, I'll take some.

SWEET-SELLER. Impossible.

BIKHNI. Then go away. Scram!

SWEET-SELLER (*after some thought*). Okay, go on, take five.

BIKHNI. Give me a rupee's worth.

The sweet-seller fills a paper bag with some sweets and hands it to her, taking the money in return. He leaves. She tucks the packet away into her cloth bundle and continues to eat her banana. A weary Sanichari enters, on her way back from the mela, carrying a bundle on her head. Her foot slips on the discarded banana peel. She falls.

SANICHARI. Hai Maiyya!

Bikhni laughs out loud. Sanichari picks herself up with difficulty. She glowers at Bikhni, then stands up. Bikhni keeps laughing loudly.

SANICHARI. Why, you idiot, does your father own this road or what? Chucking banana peels about like that!

BIKHNI. It doesn't belong to you either, for that matter! Don't you have eyes in your head to watch where you're going?

SANICHARI. You damned bitch, first you do something wrong, then you pick a fight about it!

BIKHNI. You're the bitch—and so's your mother! Comes prancing along and then wonders why she falls!

SANICHARI. Just listen to the whore! If you keep gobbling bananas and throwing peels left and right, won't people slip and fall?

BIKHNI. Let them fall! I'm going to continue eating as I like and chucking peels as I like (*she throws the second skin on the ground*).

SANICHARI. You wretch, I'll teach you a lesson . . .

Sanichari slaps Bikhni hard. Bikhni is momentarily taken aback, then she grabs hold of Sanichari's hair and they begin to fight. Suddenly Sanichari looks searchingly at Bikhni's face and stops, astounded.

SANICHARI (*wonderingly*). Kaali Kamli . . . aren't you Kaali Kamli?

BIKHNI (*taken aback*). What did you say?

SANICHARI. Aren't you Bikhni? Kaali Kamli . . . ?

BIKHNI. Who're you?

SANICHARI. Arre, I'm Sanichari—Sanichari from Tohri.

Bikhni is amazed. The two circle each other, staring at one another.

BIKHNI. Sanichari . . . you mean the daughter of Pipartala's Mangla chacha? The one with long, long nails? That Sanichari?

SANICHARI. Yes, yes, that very one.

BIKHNI. After all these years . . . in a mela . . . (*words fail her. They embrace.*) Weren't you married to someone in Tahad village?

SANICHARI. Yes. And you?

BIKHNI. In Jujubhatu . . .

SANICHARI. You've changed so much . . . become an old woman . . .

BIKHNI. What d'you expect? I am old! Look at you, you're looking pretty old too. You still remember the Kaali Kamli bit[1] . . . ?

SANICHARI. How could I forget? You'd walk around in that ghagra[2] made out of a black quilt . . .

BIKHNI. And what about your cat-like claws, with which you'd scratch us all the time . . .

SANICHARI. Arre, dhat! Look, see for yourself—no nails.

BIKHNI. Foolish creature, I no longer have that black ghagra either! (*They laugh.*) But tell me—how come you're at the mela?

SANICHARI. I came to look for my grandson.

BIKHNI. What happened to him?

SANICHARI. Let it rest. It's a long story.

BIKHNI (*lifting her bundle*). You look as if you've been out since the morning, and I bet you haven't eaten a thing all day . . .

SANICHARI. No, no, I had something at the mela . . .

BIKHNI (*taking out a roti*). What're you acting so formal for? Here, sit yourself down and have this. Go on, eat it.

SANICHARI. You have some too . . .

BIKHNI. Oh, I'm full, I've been eating non-stop. Okay, tell me, who are the family members you live with?

SANICHARI. I'm completely alone.

BIKHNI. Alone? But your husband, children . . . ?

SANICHARI. Let's not talk about me, tell me all about yourself. Weren't you married off to some blacksmith in Jujubhatu?

BIKHNI. Yes. Tell me about your grandson. What happened to him?

SANICHARI. I have no one else in my life but him, Bikhni. They've all left me one by one. He was my only hope, my

---

1. Roughly meaning—black quilted.
2. Traditional full-length gathered skirt.

only comfort. And even he quarrelled with me one day and ran away. I came here hoping to find him.

BIKHNI. Arre Sanichari, what can one do, it's all written in one's fate.

SANICHARI. I know he won't come back, but even then I keep looking for him here and there like a mad woman . . .

BIKHNI. Poor you. . . you're just unlucky, that's all . . .

SANICHARI. Tell me about yourself. What're you doing here?

BIKHNI. What can I say? My story's like yours, more or less. I have just the one son. He was born four years after my marriage, after so many wishes and prayers! He was just a baby when my husband died of a snake bite. It was a real struggle to get by—at first I reared other people's calves, then slowly managed to get four cows of my own, and two milk-yielding goats. Anyhow, I managed with great difficulty to raise my son, and finally gave him in marriage—

SANICHARI. Where?

BIKHNI. In Lohardanga. His in-laws are very well off. For his wedding, I took a loan from the mahajan[1] and feasted the whole village on dahi and chivda.

SANICHARI. Then what happened?

BIKHNI. What else? The mahajan claimed my home and everything I had as repayment. And to my misfortune, my son, lured by the wealth of his in-laws, shifted in with them as a live-in son-in-law!

SANICHARI. Didn't you try to talk to him, explain . . .

BIKHNI. Arre, I did all that. I told him, beta, let's sell our cows and goats and repay the mahajan's loan. Instead, that thieving son of mine took my cattle with him and ran off to his in-laws!

SANICHARI. My god!

BIKHNI. But I'm not to be outdone that easily. I can be just as sly. I stole back two goats and sold them at the mela. I got

---

1. Moneylender.

thirty-two rupees for them, and I took the money and set off.

SANICHARI. Where will you go now?

BIKHNI. Wherever chance takes me. Just as you have no son to call your own, I have a son who isn't really mine. I'll go off . . . to Daltongunj—Gomo—Bokaro—beg for alms on some railway station . . .

SANICHARI. You'll be a beggar?

BIKHNI. What else . . . ? (*A little boy darts on and blows a whistle in Bikhni's ear.*) Scram, you little bastard! (*The boy runs off.*)

SANICHARI. God knows what kind of unlucky star we were born under! You know, Bikhni, this is what happens when a woman doesn't have a man in her life. I tell you what—you come with me, Bikhni.

BIKHNI. Where?

SANICHARI. To my home. It's far too empty as it is . . . both of us will live there together . . .

BIKHNI. How can I . . . no, no, I can't go with you.

SANICHARI. Arre, come, please come. Don't make a fuss. Look, I live all alone. If you come and live with me, it'll cheer me up.

BIKHNI. All right. I'll come. Do you have enough water where you live? Any water problem?

SANICHARI. No, not at all—there's a whole river for our use.

BIKHNI. Okay, then let's go. But you keep these thirty rupees with you.

SANICHARI. No, no—I want you stay with me, but I won't take your money. Keep it with you. This Sanichari is still capable of getting by on her own earnings!

BIKHNI. No. If you won't take this, then I won't go with you. Go on, keep these thirty rupees with you.

Sanichari takes the money. She hoists her bundle and stands up, then extends her hand to Bikhni.

SANICHARI. Come, get up. Pick up your things.

BIKHNI. Yes, let's go. Tonight I'll miss my little grand-
daughter a lot . . .

SANICHARI. Come, let's go—bit by bit you'll forget all that . . .
They leave. The lights dim slowly.

Scene 6

*Evening. Sanichari's home. The house is looking neat and cared for,
with a freshly washed covering on the charpoy. Bikhni, seated on a low
stool, is humming to herself as she carefully oils, combs and plaits
Sanichari's hair.*

BIKHNI. Arre you wretch, what a state your hair is in!
Crawling with lice—whole fields of them!

SANICHARI. Nibbling away at me all day . . . and because of
these damned lice even my nights were ruined—I couldn't
sleep!

BIKHNI. You were messy even as a child. Those huge, long
nails; oily, uncombed hair!

SANICHARI. And what about your black ghagra! Ram, Ram! It
stank so much even dogs were scared away!

BIKHNI. Hold still, you black-tongued woman! Let me
massage the oil in properly! Here, pass me the comb.

SANICHARI. Look beside you, it must be there. (*Bikhni gets up
and fetches the comb.*) We've used up so much oil, Bikhni!

BIKHNI. Shh, sit still . . .

SANICHARI. Where did I ever get the time to do my hair or
dress up, Bikhni? My life has been nothing but the stove,
the chakki, and outside jobs. If you had been in the same
situation you would have realized . . .

BIKHNI. Oh I, of course, was lording it like a queen, feasting
on sweetmeats all day! Arre, what can you do, such is a
woman's lot . . .

SANICHARI. If my bahu[1] had been half-way decent, I would
have been better off. As it is, I divided my time between
cleaning up my in-laws' shit and piss, and tending to my

---

1. Daughter-in-law.

Budhua. My son died, my daughter-in-law ran off . . . I brought up my grandson, looked after him till he was a young man, and then he went off with the no-good magic-men . . . My whole life has been spent working, working . . .

BIKHNI. What a life! Full of tears, sorrow . . .

SANICHARI. No, I never had the time to weep. They all died, one by one. My in-laws, my brother-in-law and his wife, my husband, my son. I didn't shed a single tear. They call me a daain—say it's as if I was born just to devour others.

BIKHNI. Which son of a bitch dares call you a dain? I'll scratch his eyes out! Don't worry, Sanichari, you'll see, everything will turn out fine. I'll get hold of some fertilizer from the government office and start growing vegetables once again, and I'll sell them myself in the market.

Bikhni completes plaiting Sanichari's hair, and takes a look at her handiwork. Something strikes her. She fetches something from her bundle.

SANICHARI. What's happened?

BIKHNI. Wait a minute.

SANICHARI. What's this . . . ?

BIKHNI. Wait a bit . . . (*she puts a pair of earrings on Sanichari*) let me put it on. I had bought them at the mela for myself. Just see how nice they look!

SANICHARI. Go on with you!

BIKHNI. Stop acting coy! (*She gets up and fetches the mirror*) Go ahead, take a good look.

Sanichari casts a quick glance at herself, then, embarrassed, puts the mirror away.

SANICHARI. This is the first time in my whole life that anyone has given me a gift . . . no, no, once my husband also . . . he took me to the Baisakhi mela at Tohri. He bought me lots of red and yellow bangles, and some alta,[1] but . .

---

1. Decorative red dye for the feet.

BIKHNI. What happened?

SANICHARI. The next day I threw everything into the river, the bangles, the alta, my sindoor . . .[1]

BIKHNI. Why?

SANICHARI. He paid a rupee and bought some of the milk that had been blessed by Shivji maharaj. The milk was stale, it had gone sour . . . within three hours he got severe cholera and died right there, in the government hospital . . .

BIKHNI. My god! Cholera from sacred offerings?

SANICHARI. What else d'you expect from a poor man's god? D'you know, because I was alone, I was forced to perform two kriya ceremonies for my dead husband?

BIKHNI. Really?

SANICHARI. Really. The Tohri panda told me that since you're here, you must make the pinda offering before you go. I paid a rupee and a quarter for an offering of sand and sattu. What a to-do there was in our village panchayat over this! That bastard Mohanlal said, how can a Tohri brahmin know how we hold a kriya ceremony in Tahad village! He landed me with a second kriya ceremony. I had to feed the whole village on curds and chivda after taking a loan from Ramavatar.

BIKHNI. D'you mean to say that the brahmins of Tohri village are different from the brahmins of Tahad village?

SANICHARI. Who knows . . . the thakurs and brahmins are all in this together. They control everything. It took me five years to pay off my debt to the thakur.

BIKHNI. All these bastards are the same! (*They clean the dishes, put them away, and drink some water.*) Come, let's get some sleep.

SANICHARI. You haven't sat still a moment since you've come! You 'cleaned out the house, made cowdung cakes, picked the lice out of my hair, you want to plant the vegetable patch tomorrow morning—I'm telling you, Bikhni, in my whole life nobody has done so much for me. No one

---

1. Vermilion worn by women as a sign of marriage.

has even thought of me as a human being!

BIKHNI. Why are you keeping a tally? Whatever I've done is for us, after all—not for someone else. Go to sleep now.

SANICHARI. You know, when I was a girl my mother used to always tell me that a woman's worst enemy was other women . . .

BIKHNI. Arre, that's all stuff made up by men. Go on, go to sleep.

SANICHARI. Tonight I'll sleep peacefully . . .

They lie down beside each other and fall asleep. The light dims slowly.

Scene 7

Morning. Sanichari's home. Sanichari and Bikhni are squatting and counting their money. A pot lies beside them. Sanichari turns it upside down, and Bikhni starts to sort out the money. The counting begins.

SANICHARI. Twenty plus twenty makes forty, plus five makes forty-five and thirty and seventy-five paise—

BIKHNI. Not thirty, forty.

SANICHARI. How forty? Now look what you've done, you've mixed me up again.

BIKHNI. I've mixed you up? You've been counting all wrong from the start!

SANICHARI. Okay, wait, let me start again. Look, here's fifty paise, here's forty, that makes eighty—

BIKHNI. Arre, idiot, do forty and fifty make eighty?

SANICHARI. Yes—no, no, wait a bit (*counts on her fingers*) sixty, seventy, eighty, ninety—okay, ninety and thirty . . . that makes one rupee twenty paise, doesn't it?

BIKHNI. Yes . . .

SANICHARI. Five and five ten, plus five fifteen, and . . .

Misri enters.

MISRI. So then, Sanichari, what's happening?

Sanichari's calculations get disturbed again.

SANICHARI. Oh, we're busy making sweetmeats for your wedding, that's all—come, join us!

MISRI. Why are you so badtempered? I just came to get news of your friend here. (*To Bikhni*) How are you, sister?

SANICHARI. Got your news? Now you can leave.

MISRI. I heard that your friend brought a whole lot of money with her . . .

BIKHNI. Yes . . . a whole treasure-chest full! Can't you see? No matter how much we count, there's still more . . .

MISRI. Having fun, eh, Sanichari?

SANICHARI. Oh, yes, loads of fun. Tell you what, Misri—leave your husband and come live here with us. Then all three of us can have lots of fun . . .

MISRI. Why are you talking rubbish, Sanichari! You have a filthy mind! I just come here to ask after your friend, and you start insulting me!

SANICHARI. Run along, now. All morning she's been hovering around us! (*Misri leaves.*) She's an out-and-out bitch, that old hag! She's mixed me up completely . . . fifty and forty makes—

BIKHNI. That's enough, stop, you've done enough counting! (*She counts*) Altogether it comes to two rupees and thirty paise!

SANICHARI. Hai Maiyya! Just two rupees thirty paise! That's all that's left!

BIKHNI. What do you expect? D'you think we can live a lifetime on thirty rupees?

SANICHARI. Now what will happen?

BIKHNI. We're in trouble . . . there aren't any vegetables in the yard either.

SANICHARI. We used up all your money, Bikhni . . .

BIKHNI. What's this 'your' money business? The money was there, it got used up, that's all there is to it. (*Sanichari keeps quiet.*) You still haven't accepted me as your own, Sanichari.

Dulan's wife's voice is heard, off, raised in anger.

DULAN'S WIFE. Hai, may you die, you bastards! May you perish in flames! If I catch you, I'll roast you in the oven! Arre, why are you running away, you brats, if you have the guts come and face me! Come on!

BIKHNI. Sounds like Lachmi.

SANICHARI (*peering out*). What's happened, oh mother of Dhatua?

DULAN'S WIFE (*as she enters*). Damn brats!

SANICHARI. Why were you screaming like that? Aren't you going to tell us?

DULAN'S WIFE. Should I sit quietly and let those bastards get away with it? The next time they enter my courtyard I'll break their legs!

SANICHARI. Arre, will you tell us what happened, or are you going to keep blathering on like this?

DULAN'S WIFE. I spent hours carefully grinding the dal to make badis,[1] and put them out into the sun to harden, and those bastards came and stole them all!

SANICHARI. Who? Who stole them?

DULAN'S WIFE. Hanumanji's descendants, those damned monkeys!

BIKHNI. Monkeys . . . ? You mean all this time you've been carrying on about monkeys! (*she laughs*).

DULAN'S WIFE. What're you grinning about? If that marauding army of bastards had laid your vegetable patch to waste you would know how it feels . . .

DULAN (*entering*). Arre, why are you cursing Ramji's disciples so roundly?

DULAN'S WIFE. Now don't you start! All my hard work . . .

SANICHARI (*arranging the charpoy*). All right, now calm down.

BIKHNI. We'll make you some more badis.

---

1. A spicy concoction of ground dal balls.

SANICHARI. Come, sit down, Dulan. It's good that you're here. Only you can help us.

DULAN. Now what's the matter?

SANICHARI. What can I say? All our savings are gone. There are no vegetables to sell. From tomorrow we'll have to starve.

DULAN. Why should you starve when there are so many ways to earn a living?

BIKHNI. It's the malik-mahajans who have ways of earning open to them. Us dushads and ganjus have to make our own openings.

DULAN. So go ahead and make them. Across the river there's a road being built for the Devi's temple. Dhatua was telling me that they're looking for labourers. Go there with your friend and set to work.

DULAN'S WIFE. In your dotage you're losing whatever little brains you had! You expect them to break stones at their age!

DULAN. Arre, if they can't break stones, they can pick one up, can't they?

SANICHARI. What do you mean?

DULAN. Early in the morning, when there's no one about, when everyone's sleeping, quietly make your way to the river and pick up a black stone from the riverbank.

SANICHARI. A black stone?

DULAN. Let me finish. Then you wash and bathe that stone, anoint it with oil, put sindoor on it and take your place in the Tohri market place.

SANICHARI. Then?

DULAN. Then? Then you announce to everyone that Mahavirji visited you in your dreams and granted you a vision. Wait and see how the devout will throng to make offerings to your stone!

BIKHNI. This is a fine opening you've shown us, Dulan! We'll rake in the money!

SANICHARI. Quiet! Making mockery of the gods! All my life I've worked hard to earn my living—and now, in my old age, am I to fool around like this with something sacred?!

DULAN. Well, you can consider it fooling around, or mockery, if you wish. But it just shows that you have a wicked mind. That's why you see something sinful wherever you look.

SANICHARI. How come?

DULAN. How come? I'll tell you. Now, you know Lachman's old mother has joint pains, don't you?

SANICHARI. Yes, she does.

DULAN. That old woman handed me ten rupees and said— Dulan bhaiya, fetch me some of Deviji's oil from the market, won't you? I said okay; but who's going to go haring off to the market just for that old hag? Two days later I took some oil from home and handed it to her. She applied that oil and a couple of days later that same bedridden old creature was hopping gaily all over the village on her own two legs. . .

BIKHNI. You save your tallest tales for us old women, huh, Dulan?

DULAN. I swear on Ram bhagwan that every word is god's own truth. Arre, if your mind is pure then your actions are pure! I'm telling you, Sanichari, no god is more important than your belly. One does whatever it takes to feed one's stomach.

An agitated Bijua enters.

BIJUA. Dulan bhaiya, arre oh, Dulan bhaiya!

DULAN. What's the matter? What's happened?

BIJUA. Arre, there's a big to-do in the village! Bhairo Singh of Barohi village has been murdered!

WOMEN (*together*). Hai Ram!

DULAN. What're you saying . . . ?

BIJUA. Yes, bhaiya. This morning at daybreak Bhairo

Singh's corpse was found lying in the middle of the fields.

DULAN. What . . .?

BIJUA. And the murderer is his son Madho Singh.

DULAN. Really?

BIJUA. That's what the villagers all say.

SANICHARI. Hai Maiyya!

BIKHNI. What a world this is—a son killing his father . . .

BIJUA. The world of the wealthy is different from ours. For the sake of money, a mother can kill her son, a son his mother.

DULAN. Achha, has Madho Singh been caught yet?

BIJUA. Are you crazy? Will the police arrest someone like him? These people have the power of money—the law, the police, the government, are all firmly in their grasp.

SANICHARI. Bhairo Singh may have died, but your luck has blossomed . . .

BIJUA. Why not! Just wait and see what a fancy kriya ceremony Madho Singh will arrange for his father! Already two and a half maunds of sandalwood, pure ghee and incense have been sent for. Know what, Dulan bhaiya, he's even sent for whores to wail at the funeral!

DULAN. Really?

BIJUA. Okay, I'm off. I still have to inform Mohanlal—I thought I'd stop off on the way and tell you people first. Okay, I'm going now, bhaiya (*leaves hastily*).

SANICHARI. Arre Bijua, at least have a glass of water—

BIJUA (*over his shoulder*). No, no, bhauji, some other time.

DULAN. How about it, Sanichari?

SANICHARI. What . . . ?

DULAN. Arre, a thakur has died, mourners are bound to be required. Do one thing, the two of you present yourselves—

BIKHNI. Are there no family members to weep for him?

DULAN. Only the families of the poor mourn their dead. The

rich households have to hire mourners. Arre, if you mourn for them you'll get money, grain, and the day after the kriya you'll even get clothes and a good meal.

SANICHARI. Hai Maiyya, are you suggesting that I should mourn? Me? I haven't been able to shed a tear, ever. When Budhua's father died, I thought at least then I would really cry hard. I even went and sat under a peepul tree and all day I kept thinking now I'll cry, now I'll cry—then it became evening and I hadn't shed a single tear.

DULAN. Arre, that's not the kind of crying I'm talking of. This is crying for money, crying as a business. Just do it the way you would grind wheat or carry bricks for the sake of a daily wage.

BIKHNI. Take me to them, Dulan, I can cry magnificently!

DULAN'S WIFE. Couldn't you think of some other work for them than sitting and mourning alongside cheap whores!

DULAN. Hold your tongue. A job's a job. You two come along, I'll take you there. The better the mourners, the more the malik's prestige increases.

SANICHARI. What will people say, Dulan?

BIKHNI. Are people going to come and feed us, support us? (*To Dulan*) Come, Dulan, I'm ready to go.

SANICHARI. But . . . Bikhni . . .

BIKHNI. Shush. Go on, old man, tell us when you'll take us along.

DULAN. I'll come to fetch you in the afternoon. Be sure to wear black. And listen, Sanichari—I want my share of your earnings from any job I arrange for you.

SANICHARI. You so-and-so, you want a cut, do you!

DULAN. So what's wrong with that? Everyone from the Prime Minister down to the lowest untouchable takes cuts.

BIKHNI. A hundred bastards must have died to give birth to a rascal like you . . .

Lights off.

Scene 8

Afternoon. The courtyard of Bhairo Singh's mansion. Mohanlal pandit is reciting from the Gita. On one side, some boys are splitting bamboos. A cluster of prostitutes is busy laughing and giggling. Bhairo Singh's corpse is laid out on the ground, covered with a white sheet. Bachha Singh is seated by its feet. Madho Singh enters with a diya.[1] He sits beside Mohanlal. After completing his recitation of the shlokas, Mohanlal begins the pinda dan ceremony.[2]

MOHANLAL. Now say after me—for the purity of my father's soul I make an offering to the brahmin—

MADHO SINGH. I make an offering—

MOHANLAL. Of a set of clothes . . .

MADHO SINGH. A set of clothes . .

MOHANLAL. Of grain . . .

MADHO SINGH. Of grain . . .

MOHANLAL. Now repeat after me—for the purity of my father's soul I gift the brahmin a bed complete with bedclothes. . .

MADHO SINGH. I gift a bed . . .

Mohanlal looks around him, and gets annoyed when he doesn't see a bed.

MOHANLAL. Arre, where's the gift of a bed?

MADHO SINGH (*bounding to his feet*). What the hell, Bijua, Bachanlal, where's the bed?

BIJUA. Huzoor, it's been loaded onto the bullock cart.

The women laugh loudly.

MOHANLAL. Calm down, Madho Singhji, calm down. Come, sit (*Madho Singh sits again*). Now make the final offering. Say—for the purity of my father's soul I gift the brahmin a cow . . .

---

1. Small clay lamp.
2. Pinda dan: a ritual in which the offspring prays for the peace of the departed parent's soul.

MADHO SINGH. I gift a cow . . .

MOHANLAL (*to Bijua*). Hey, Bijua, is the cow outside?

BIJUA. Why are you so worried, panditji? Everything's there.

MOHANLAL. All right, all right (*to Madho Singh*). Now
sprinkle holy water seven times to purify the dead soul.
(*Madho Singh sprinkles the corpse with holy water while Mohanlal
recites the shloka.*) 'Om apavitraha pavitro va sarva vastahag
todipva/yoh smaret pundri kakshayam sa brahma
bhyantarah shuchiha.' The first pinda dan in this family
now comes to an end. Now please get up, Madho Singhji,
touch your father's feet and depart. (*Madho Singh follows the
instructions and leaves.*)

BACHANLAL. Is everything done, panditji?

MOHANLAL. Yes, bhaiya, everything's done.

*Bachanlal also exits. Mohanlal is busy gathering up his things. A
boy enters carrying a bundle of blankets on his head.*

BOY. Where shall I put these blankets? They're meant to be
donated to the doms.[1]

BIJUA. Put them inside, where else?

MOHANLAL (*busy gathering together his things*). So Bijua, have you
arranged for the fresh milk?

BIJUA. Right away, panditji.

He goes in. The prostitutes begin to tease the pandit.

PROSTITUTE 1. Why, panditji, that's a lot of stuff you've
gathered . . .

PROSTITUTE 2. Panditji, how come you didn't ask for a radio
in your list of donations?

PROSTITUTE 3. When you're sleeping beside your wife on that
thousand rupee bed I hope you'll arrange for some song
and dance as well!

They laugh raucously. The pandit gets annoyed.

MOHANLAL (*in anger*). Quiet! How dare you! You've been

---

1. Doms are untouchables who handle corpses and work in cremation
grounds.

brought here to mourn, and you sit there cackling your heads off!

Bijua enters with the milk. One of the prostitutes tugs at his dhoti and addresses him.

PROSTITUTE 2. Hey there, Bijua, how come we don't see you in the neighbourhood nowadays? Found greener pastures, have you? (*They all laugh loudly.*)

BIJUA. Dhat! (*He frees his dhoti and approaches the pandit.*) Here, panditji, here's the fresh milk.

MOHANLAL. Okay, leave it here.

Bachanlal enters.

BACHANLAL. Panditji, here's fifty-one rupees for the priest's fee. (*Mohanlal takes the money and is about to leave*) Bijua, load all panditji's goods onto the cart. (*Bijua picks up the things and prepares to follow the pandit out. Bachanlal tells the pandit*) Be sure to come early for the fourth day ceremony. Don't be late.

MOHANLAL (*turns as he is leaving*). Don't worry about that, I'll be here for sure. But Bachanlalji, don't forget my button-down umbrella . . .

BACHANLAL. Okay, okay, it'll be arranged.

MOHANLAL. Fine.

He exits, with Bijua behind him, carrying his things.

BACHANLAL. How much longer now?

NATUA. It's almost done, sarkar.[1]

He ties the rope. A boy enters with a tin of ghee.

SANKAR. Sarkar, where should I put this?

BACHANLAL. On my head, you idiot!

SANKAR. Oh . . .

BACHANLAL. Go inside and hand it to the young mistress. (*He looks at the prostitutes, and notices that they aren't wailing.*) You haven't the least consideration for your master's

---

1. Term of respect.

honour! All your life you've been fed, clothed and
pampered by him! And now you shameless hussies can't
shed a tear at his passing!

PROSTITUTE. Yes, yes, the master was like a god to us! He
made whores of us, fed and clothed us and on his death left
us five whole rupees! How can we not mourn him! Come
on, let's start! (*They begin to wail.*)

Bijua enters.

BACHANLAL. Hey, Bijua, I asked you to organize ten or fifteen
good rudalis, and all you could arrange was these three
withered hags!

PROSTITUTE. The good ones can earn more than your measly
five rupees on the job, why would they come here to beat
their breasts!

BACHANLAL. You're getting too big for your boots—shut up
and keep· crying.

OLD PROSTITUTE. If you don't give us something to eat and
drink how do you expect us to keep crying?

BACHANLAL. Shut up, old woman, first do your job!

Madho Singh enters.

MADHO SINGH. Well, Bachanlal—

BACHANLAL. Yes, sarkar?

MADHO SINGH. How much longer? Will the corpse be carried
out before the sun goes down, or not? (*Looking at Bachcha
Singh*). What are you sitting here for, pulling a long face?
Go, change your clothes and get ready.

BACHANLAL. We're only waiting for Lachman babu, sarkar.

MADHO SINGH. The sandalwood logs and ghee and so on are
ready . . .

BACHANLAL. Yes, sarkar.

MADHO SINGH. When the pyre is set alight, I want it to be
known for miles around that Madho Singh's father is
being cremated.

BACHANLAL. Don't worry, sarkar, all the arrangements have

been made perfectly.

MADHO SINGH. My father was the head of all the thakurs of Birohi village. His kriya ceremony should be as grand as an emperor's. Money's no problem—don't stint on anything. (*He turns to leave, then suddenly sees the three rudalis. He stops.*) What's this, only three rudalis? (*Loudly*) Arre, Madho Singh's father dies and you arrange just three rudalis? Why didn't you get the whole whores' quarter here?

BACHANLAL. Sarkar, I kept telling Bijua the barber—

MADHO SINGH. Where's that son of a bitch? Send for the bastard!

BACHANLAL. Bijua!!

Bijua comes running.

BIJUA. Yes, sarkar . . .

MADHO SINGH. What the hell, you fucker! D'you think it's your father who's dead, that you've picked up these three deadbeats?

BIJUA. Huzoor, they . . .

MADHO SINGH. Shut up, you shit! Not a word out of you! Send someone to the whores' quarter! I want the whole redlight district to report here, understand?

BIJUA. Yes, sarkar (*he leaves*).

MADHO SINGH. Madho Singh's father's funeral, and only three . . . (*he breaks down and sobs. Puts a hanky to his eyes*) Babuji![1] (*He can't speak.*)

Natua enters with the bamboo stretcher for the body.

PROSTITUTE. The bastard murders his own father and then weeps crocodile tears!

BIJUA (*entering on the run*). Sarkar, Lachman babu's here.

Lachman Singh enters.

LACHMAN. Madho my son!

---

1. Father!

MADHO SINGH. Chachaji! (*He touches the older man's feet.*)

PROSTITUTE 1. Lachman Singh of Tahad.

PROSTITUTE 2. Another one for the whores.

LACHMAN SINGH. Take yourself in hand, my son. People come, people go—that's the way of the world. I've had a word with the Darogaji,[1] my son. Bachcha Singh, come here. (*Bachcha Singh gets up and goes to him. To Madho*) Now you'll have to look after him.

MADHO SINGH. You don't have to be concerned, chachaji, he's my responsibility now.

BACHCHA SINGH. What's happened to my father?

LACHMAN SINGH. An enemy murdered him, my son.

BACHCHA SINGH. Will he kill me too?

LACHMAN SINGH. No, no my son. Your brother will look after you well—isn't that so, Madho?

MADHO SINGH. Don't worry about a thing, chachaji.

LACHMAN SINGH. Let me take a last look at my brother . . . (*He begins to remove the white sheet covering the corpse but Madho Singh hurriedly stops him.*)

MADHO SINGH. You won't be able to stand it, chachaji. He's really been hacked up. Come, let's go (*leads him away*).

LACHMAN SINGH (*as he's led away*). You come along as well, Bachcha Singh.

They exit. Bachanlal goes up to scold the rudalis.

BACHANLAL. What the hell, have you been brought here to recite the scriptures? Go on, wail your loudest. Letting me down in front of the master!

Dulan enters with Sanichari and Bikhni.

DULAN. Ram Ram, Bachan bhaiya!

BACHANLAL. How are you, Dulan?

DULAN. I was so upset to hear that the old master was no

---

1. Police officer.

more, that I decided to bring along two rudalis. After all, he deserves a really grand kriya ceremony!

The prostitutes stop wailing and nudge each other.

BACHANLAL. All right, tell the two of them to sit beside them. (*To Sanichari and Bikhni*) Here, sit.

DULAN. Sarkar, first the payment terms . . .

BACHANLAL. What terms do you expect for these old hags?

DULAN. Sarkar, these women may look old, but wait till you hear them mourn! You'll find yourself shedding tears!

BACHAN. Okay, they'll get some grain.

DULAN. That's not enough, sarkar. I've heard that a full two hundred rupees have been allocated just for rudalis.

BACHANLAL. Okay, okay, five rupees as well.

DULAN. Only five rupees! For women from decent homes! You must give them at least twenty rupees each, sarkar.

BACHANLAL. Are you mad? Twenty rupees each?! Okay, you can take thirty for the two of them. That's all.

DULAN. Thirty rupees, rice and clothes.

BACHANLAL. Not rice, wheat.

DULAN. Give them rice, sarkar. They've got good, strong voices.

BACHANLAL. Dulan, how many bastards died to give birth to you?

DULAN. Twenty-two, sarkar . . .

BACHANLAL. Hey, Natua, is the bamboo stretcher ready or not?

PROSTITUTE. God knows where he picked up these two. Can these old hags cry?

Sanichari and Bikhni break into dramatic wails and cries as they approach the corpse. As they mourn loudly, slowly people begin to enter and gather around. As soon as Madho Singh comes in, Bachanlal goes up to him.

BACHANLAL. Didn't I tell you not to worry, sarkar?

*The crying and wailing reaches a climax. While crying, Sanichari
and Bikhni fall on each others' necks. Bachha Singh, affected by
this, begins to cry aloud as he beats his head on his father's corpse.*

BACHHA SINGH. Bappa . . . Bappa!¹

*Madho Singh tries to quieten him.
The lights dim slowly.*

Scene 9

*Sanichari's home. A winter evening. The house is looking a little more
prosperous than before. There are a few additional household items.
Sanichari and Bikhni enter. They are dressed in black ghagras. Bikhni
is carrying a large bundle. Sanichari has her head covered with a
black cloth. As soon as they enter, they begin to take off the black
clothing, and drape it on the upended charpoy They sit on the ground.*

BIKHNI. Is it still hurting?

SANICHARI. Less than before. Want to eat something?

BIKHNI. Don't I just, my stomach's growling with hunger.
Go, fetch the thalis.² (*Sanichari fetches the plates while Bikhni
opens up the bundle.*) Arre, baap re, what a lot of puris and
laddus they've given us!

SANICHARI. Eat your fill. It's not every day that Nathuni
Singh's mother dies! Here (*hands Bikhni some food*).

BIKHNI. Again you've served me first . . .

SANICHARI. Arre, eat up! Just look at how much chivda and
gur we've got!

BIKHNI (*takes a roll of black cloth from the bundle*). The cloth is
really good and soft, too.

SANICHARI. In these two months we've collected so much
cloth! What shall we do with it, Bikhni?

BIKHNI. Don't worry about it. I'll take it to the market and
sell it all off . . .

---

1. Father! Father!
2. Metal dish to eat off.

SANICHARI. There's so much food. Why don't we call Dhatua's mother and share some with her?

BIKHNI (*eating*). Yes, let's do that.

SANICHARI (*going to the door*). Arre oh, mother of Dhatua!

DULAN'S WIFE. What is it?

SANICHARI. Just come here a moment . . . quick . . .

DULAN'S WIFE. Coming!

Sanichari returns to her place and sits down.

SANICHARI. Nathuni Singh really spent generously on his mother's kriya ceremony. Sandalwood, pure ghee, donations of clothing for the poor . . . Bijua was saying he spent a full thirty thousand rupees on it all!

BIKHNI. Yes, he spent thirty thousand and got thirty lakhs in return—by way of inheritance . . .

DULAN'S WIFE (*enters*). Why were you calling me?

SANICHARI. Arre, come and sit!

DULAN'S WIFE (*sitting down*). So what did your fortune bring you today?

BIKHNI. What can it bring us? We split our foreheads open mourning at Nathuni Singh's.

SANICHARI. Arre, that's all part of the business . . . here (*she gives Dulan's wife some laddu*), eat this.

DULAN'S WIFE. The laddu is good today. But Sanichari, that laddu you got day before yesterday was really stale! It stank!

BIKHNI. That's because this laddu is from the house of thakur Nathuni Singh, and that was from the house of Ganpathlal Lala. That bastard is the biggest miser going.

SANICHARI. Do you know what Lala's son Jaggilal did? In order to save money, he used dalda instead of real ghee to burn his father's corpse!

DULAN'S WIFE. Hai Maiyya!

SANICHARI. He also approached us to lower our rates, saying, take only five rupees from me, even though I know you take twenty rupees from the others! But you have to cry as well as

you would for a thakur family! I told him straight,
mourning a death is not like trading in oil or salt, that
you can bargain and haggle! Huh! Trying to compete with
the thakurs!

BIKHNI. We told him plainly—not a paisa less than fifty
rupees!

DULAN'S WIFE. Well done! The stingy old miser!

Misri enters.

MISRI. Hai Maiyya! Hogging laddus, I see, mother of Dhatua!

Dhatua's wife enters alongside.

DHATUA'S WIFE. Maai, chachi's looking for you . . .

DULAN'S WIFE. What is it, Misri?

MISRI. Shall I come in so's I can tell you?

BIKHNI. No. You stay there. (*She gives Dhatua's wife some laddu*)
Here, have some. (*She gets up and goes to Misri with some laddu
in her hand*) Go on, your ladyship, you can hog some as well
(*she starts to give her some, then snatches back her hand*) oh, oh,
wait, let me just ask Sanichari—(*turns and asks Sanichari*).
What d'you say, Sanichari, shall we give her some?
(*Sanichari inclines her head in assent.*)

MISRI (*taking the laddu from her*). Sanichari, your luck has really
turned! Feasting on halwa-puri every day!

BIKHNI. How does it bother you? Is it your father's wealth?

MISRI. Arre, when my father died, we really ate well! And
this one—her father died, her husband died, but the
woman never so much as shed a tear! Why should she,
after all—there was no halwa-puri to be had, was there?

BIKHNI. You've eaten your laddu, now get out of here.

MISRI. I only came because my cow's giving birth, I'm not
interested in anyone's laddus! (*she leaves.*)

DHATUA'S WIFE. Don't let her depress you, chachi. Nothing
can change her twisted mind.

An old woman enters.

WOMAN. Does Sanichari live here?

Bikhni gets up and goes to her. The old woman whispers in her ear.

BIKHNI. Hey, Sanichari, just come here a moment . . .

Sanichari goes up to them. The three of them talk softly, then the old woman leaves. Dulan's wife gestures to her daughter-in-law.

DULAN'S WIFE. Arre oh Sanichari, what's up?

SANICHARI. Nathuni Singh's middle wife is here.

DULAN'S WIFE. What? Mohar Singh's daughter here, in your home? Okay, we'd better be off.

BIKHNI. Arre, sit for a while. Take some chivda with you.

DULAN'S WIFE. I'll take some in the evening. Besides, there's Misri's cow to be seen to. (*To her daughter-in-law*) Come, let's go.

They leave. Sanichari picks up the bundle and other things and goes in. Bikhni arranges the charpoy for a visitor. Sanichari brings out a covering and lays it on the charpoy. The thakurain enters.

SANICHARI. Please sit down, thakurain.

Bikhni fetches a pot of water and a napkin. She washes the thakurain's feet and wipes them with the cloth, then touches her feet as a gesture of respect. The old attendant enters and seats herself at the back.

SANICHARI. Huzoorain, you here . . . ?

THAKURAIN. I have something urgent to tell you.

BIKHNI. You could have sent for us, why did you go to the trouble of coming here?

THAKURAIN. You'll have to take the early morning bus to Lohri village tomorrow.

SANICHARI. Why Lohri village, thakurain?

THAKURAIN. My father Mohar Singh has been suffering from smallpox for a month. Since last night his condition has become very serious. There's no hope for him now.

BIKHNI. But I thought only the poor got that disease?

SANICHARI. Didn't he receive any treatment?

THAKURAIN. What can I say? My mother believes in prayers

and pujas, nothing else. I have no one else but my father.
Everyone in my in-laws' home is my enemy.

SANICHARI. But your father's still alive . . .

THAKURAIN. In name only. Such a pampered body, fed on
milk and ghee, that his soul just doesn't want to leave it!
Ten villages used to quake at the sound of my father Mohar
Singh's name! When he dies, I'll show them all what a
kriya ceremony is!

BIKHNI. But even Nathuni babu didn't spare any expense for
his mother's kriya. That's what a son should be like! A
real Sarvan Kumar. [1]

THAKURAIN. Son my foot! Despatched his mother to a
wretched hut near the cowshed and left her there to die.
All he did by way of treatment was to tether a goat beside
her. No question of a hakim or vaid or doctor.[2]

SANICHARI. To think that the daughter of Parakaram Singh
was reduced to this!

THAKURAIN. All day long his old mother would lie rotting
in her own piss and shit, while her son counted the days
till the old woman popped off and he could lay his hands
on all her wealth!

BIKHNI. Didn't he make any arrangements for her to be
nursed or looked after?

THAKURAIN. Yes—Motiya Dushadin and Jagna Mehtar.
Suddenly the question of her losing caste on being touched
by dushads and bhangis was no longer a problem![3] Arre,
it's all part of that older bahu's evil plan—as it is she
swaggers around all day brandishing her thick bunch of
keys and making everyone dance to her bidding.

BIKHNI. Why? Don't you have some authority too? After all,
you're the middle wife.

THAKURAIN. What authority would I have? Have I produced a
son and heir for their family? I gave birth to a daughter,
that was my big crime. When my mother-in-law died,

---

1. A legendary figure of the perfect son.
2. Hakims and vaids are doctors of indigenous systems of medicine.
3. Untouchable castes.

thirty thousand rupees were spent on her kriya. Half of that money was given by my father, but even after that they treated me badly. I refuse to stay there any longer. I'll go to my father's house, and I'll organize such a magnificent kriya for him that the whole community will talk of nothing else. Tell me, how much do I pay you?

Bikhni and Sanichari exchange looks. Sanichari gestures to Bikhni.

BIKHNI. Well, if we're to prostrate ourselves on the ground while wailing, then it's fifty rupees, and if we're to beat our breasts all the way to the cremation ground then it'll be sixty-five, and—

THAKURAIN. I'll pay a full hundred rupees, but you must raise such a ruckus that the whole village gets to know of it.

SANICHARI. But the senior mistress gave us oil, salt, chillies and dal as well.

THAKURAIN. I'll also give you rice, dal, gur, oil, salt and a thali made of brass.

BIKHNI. Clothes . . .?

THAKURAIN. Why are you so worried, you'll get everything. Just come along early in the morning. And no one should know that I came here today . . .

BIKHNI. Oh, no, huzoorain. Rest assured, no one will get to know.

They both touch her feet. She leaves along with her attendant.

SANICHARI. The rich are really strange! Just see how she came running to us as soon as she needed us for something!

BIKHNI. Arre Sanichari, we've bruised our foreheads and rent our hair mourning for others; will there be anyone to mourn for us when we die?

SANICHARI. Of course there will be! The jackals will howl for us, the hyenas and dogs will howl for us . . . Come on, let's get our things together for tomorrow morning.

Sanichari picks up the kneading dish and goes in. Bikhni upends the charpoy.

BIKHNI. Oh, Sanichari!

SANICHARI. Yes?

BIKHNI. Nothing.

SANICHARI (*putting down the dish*). Arre, what is it? Tell me.

BIKHNI. Early tomorrow morning we have to go to Mohar
  Singh's . . .

SANICHARI. So?

BIKHNI. Well, I was just thinking . . . from there I could take
  the Ranchi bus to Jujubhatu . . .

SANICHARI. What for?

BIKHNI. My brother-in-law's daughter is getting married. It's
  like this—yesterday when I went to the market, I
  happened to meet my brother-in-law. He was very insistent
  that I should go, and I also thought that this way I could get
  to see my grandchild once again . . .

SANICHARI. Two days have passed, and you didn't say a word
  to me . . .

BIKHNI. I thought it would upset you . . .

SANICHARI. You will come back, though . . . ?

BIKHNI. Why are you talking like this? This is my home,
  after all, how can I not come back!

SANICHARI. But . . . there's your grandchild . . .

BIKHNI. I'll just meet her and be back in two days, that's all.

SANICHARI. All right, go—but don't sit on a seat when you
  take the bus, they'll charge you eight rupees. Just sit on the
  floor and hand them two rupees. And listen, don't you stuff
  yourself full of rubbish on the way . . .

BIKHNI. Okay.

SANICHARI. Now go to sleep.

BIKHNI. And you . . .?

SANICHARI. I have a lot of things to do.

  *She goes in, then covers Bikhni with a covering sheet. Bikhni
  hesitates, puzzled. The lights dim.*

Scene 10

Sanichari is seated on the floor, sorting clothes, with a big bundle of cloth beside her. She picks out some thin black cloth, gets up and fetches the sewing box, then stitches the cloth. She gets up, drinks some water, sits down again. The thread is used up. It is too dark for her to thread the needle. She gets up again, checks one of the old pots, then sits down again. Dulan's voice is heard, off.

DULAN. Sanichari! Oh, Sanichari!

Sanichari gets up and opens the outer door. Dulan enters.

DULAN. The sun's gone down, how come you haven't lighted your stove?

SANICHARI. There's a roti still lying uneaten from this morning. I don't feel like cooking twice a day just for myself. (*Getting up*) Come, sit down . . .

DULAN. Let it be. (*As he sits*) Your friend seems to have disappeared . . .

SANICHARI. When she left she said she'd be back in two days. But it's been six days now, and there's no news of her.

DULAN. Arre, she won't be back. Why should she leave her son, her daughter-in-law, her grandchild, to come back here? What for?

SANICHARI. No, no, Dulan. She'll definitely come back. When she left she vowed she would. And she has a business here, why shouldn't she come back?

DULAN. Arre, if her son supports her why should she work? Anyway, I have some news for you. You've heard of thakur Gambhir Singh of Naugad, haven't you?

SANICHARI. Who hasn't? The long-nosed Gambhir Singh who used to parade through the Diwali mela on elephant-back!

DULAN. A big zamindar—lord of five villages. He really lived it up, drinking, womanizing—and now, in his old age, he's paying the price for it.

SANICHARI. Why, what's happened to him?

DULAN. What d'you expect? His entire body's rotted away. Swollen like a drum. He could drop dead any moment. Last night they even lowered his body to the ground, and this morning they found him breathing again! But the old man's time has come.

SANICHARI. So why're you telling me all this?

DULAN. Because you'll have to go when it's time to mourn. He's put it in writing that he wants a lakh of rupees to be spent on his death ceremonies. He wants to wash away all the sins of a lifetime with a lakh of rupees!

SANICHARI. But how can I go alone . . . ? Bikhni isn't here . . .

DULAN. Arre, if you sit around waiting for Bikhni you'll starve to death. I'm telling you, his kriya is going to be a really grand affair! Three different kinds of bands, horses, elephants, grain and cloth being distributed to the people of all five villages—Sanichari, you'll make enough to eat off for six months! And of course, I'll get something out of it . . .

SANICHARI. You've grown greedy for money, Dulan, you're not thinking about me. Bikhni isn't here, how can I go alone to mourn . . . ?

DULAN. Why? You can go to the whores' quarter in Tohri—at the sound of Gambhir Singh's name fifty whores will be willing to come along. And then your Parbatia is there as well . . .

SANICHARI. I? Go to the whores' quarter? To Parbatia?

DULAN. For the sake of money you can do anything. Besides, it's Gambhir Singh's own wish that whores from the whores' quarter come to mourn him at his kriya ceremony.

SANICHARI. He expects the very women whose lives he ruined to cry over his corpse?!

DULAN. Don't concern yourself with all that! Just think about your own business. Tomorrow you should go to Tohri and fix it all up. I'll take you.

Dulan leaves. Sanichari continues to sit silently. She starts to fold the black clothes. A voice is heard outside.

VOICE (*off*). Is anyone home?

SANICHARI. Who is it?

VOICE (*off*). I've come from Jujubhatu.

Sanichari eagerly goes to the outer door. A man enters.

SANICHARI. Bikhni hasn't come . . . ?

MAN. Well . . .

SANICHARI. What is it? Has something happened to her?

MAN. On her way . . . in the bus . . . she ate some fritters . . . and even after the wedding, she ate a whole lot of stale tit-bits . . .

SANICHARI. It was a bad habit of hers . . .

MAN. Well, she got cholera from eating all that . . . she passed away two days later.

SANICHARI. Didn't you have her treated?

MAN. We tried our best to persuade her to go to the hospital, but she just wouldn't agree . . .

SANICHARI. Is it that she wouldn't agree, or did fear of the expense keep you from taking her?

MAN. Did my aunt leave any of her things here?

SANICHARI. Why d'you want to know?

MAN. I'm her younger nephew . . . she was very fond of me, so I thought . . .

SANICHARI. When your aunt was roaming the streets alone with no one to help her, where were you then? (*Pause*) Run along with you. If you leave now, you can catch the eight o' clock bus.

The nephew glares at her angrily, then storms out. Sanichari shuts the door behind him. She turns and begins to fold the black clothes and place them on the cot. All at once she breaks down. Harsh sobs tear through her. Gradually the intensity of the weeping eases. She gets up slowly, and begins to fold the clothes again. The lights dim.

Scene 11

*The whores' quarter. Morning. At stage left Gangu, Champa and Sukhi
are sitting, playing Snakes and Ladders, a board game. At stage right,
a prostitute is seated, painting her nails. A transistor radio is blaring
songs from a little stool. One woman is plucking out her grey hairs as
she looks in a hand-held mirror. Two women are hanging saris up to
dry.*

CHAMPA. Three . . . three . . . three . . . (*rolls the dice*) there, I
    got three! Dhat, it's four, not three!

GANGU (*yelling*). Four means you're in the serpent's mouth! Go
    on, down you go, all the way do-ow-n!

CHAMPA. What d'you mean, in the serpent's mouth, you
    cheat! Look, look properly—four moves bring me here!

GANGU. Rubbish! Gangu isn't a cheat like you! Here, it's my
    turn to roll.

*She rolls the dice. From behind, one of the women hanging saris
speaks up.*

WOMAN. Arre, the water will finish, go and have your baths.
    You've been playing that game all morning!

SUKHI. Yes, yes, we're going, madam pandit. Why don't you
    finish washing your clothes first? (*She rolls the dice*) There,
    I've reached a nice long ladder! Pitter patter pitter patter
    right to the top! Just like Kalua the pimp hoists Gulbadan
    right up to the sky!

GANGU. Jealous, are you? Go on, go on, it's your turn next.

*Nasiban, an old maidservant, enters, carrying a kettle of tea. She
approaches the woman who is plucking out her grey hairs.*

NASIBAN. Arre, how many can you remove? There'll be more
    tomorrow! Here, take your tea. And here's your twenty-five
    paise. Don't say later that I didn't return it to you!

*She pours out tea for the women playing and sits down to watch the
game.*

CHAMPA (*yelling*). That's it! I've won, I've reached Home! You
    two can carry on struggling, I'm off to have my bath.

Gulbadan enters.

GULBADAN. Hey, Nasiban, give me some tea.

Nasiban, bringing her the tea, knocks against the mirror.

NASIBAN. Arre, why are you sitting right in the middle blocking the way? Go do this in your room.

NAILPOLISH WOMAN. So, Gulbadan, did you manage to get enough sleep?

GULBADAN (*stretching*). No, how could I? Here, Nasiban, give me another cup . . .

NAILPOLISH WOMAN. When did the bastard leave?

GULBADAN. Arre, he brought me silver buttons and started begging and pleading . . . I took pity on him . . . Hey you, why're you raising such a ruckus?!

GANGU. There—there—there—straight into the longest snake's mouth!

CHAMPA. Down you go, all the way down!

GULBADAN. What's all the noise about? (*Suddenly her eye falls on the ribbon in Champa's hair. She grabs hold of it*) Why, you thief, you've been swiping things again!

CHAMPA. Swiping what?

GULBADAN. The bitch is always stealing from others and then acting innocent. This ribbon! Did your husband give it to you?

CHAMPA. Why you liar, I brought it in the market!

GULBADAN. Market my ass! Take it off this minute, you bitch! Go on, take it off!

Gulbadan grabs Champa by the hair and drags her across the stage. The other women try to separate them. Meanwhile Sanichari enters.

SANICHARI. Can someone tell me if Parbatia lives here?

GULBADAN (*noticing Sanichari*). What d'you want?

GANGU. Arre, I know you—weren't you one of the rudalis at Bhairo Singh's? Where's the other one, your friend?

SAEEDA. Arre baap re baap, how they cried! I still haven't forgotten it!

GULBADAN. No one's died here, what have you come here for?

SANICHARI. I want to meet Parbatia.

GULBADAN. There's no Parbatia here—

CHAMPA. Why are you lying? Doesn't that Parbatia from Tahad village stay here? Wait, I'll just call her.

GANGU. Why don't you sit down? (*gives her a stool*). Arre oh, Nasiban, bring some tea! (*To Sanichari*) What's your name?

SANICHARI. Sanichari . . .

SAEEDA. What do you want with Parbatia?

Nasiban brings the tea and hands it to Sanichari.

GANGU. Here, have your tea.

As Nasiban hands over the tea, Parbatia enters, drying her long, wet hair.

PARBATIA. The bitch didn't even let me bathe in peace—who the hell is it? Showing up at this odd hour! (*As she throws back her hair she sees Sanichari*) What are you doing here?

SANICHARI. I have something urgent to talk to you about.

PARBATIA. There's nothing I want to hear from you. Go away.

SANICHARI. You haven't changed a bit! I came here to help you . . .

PARBATIA. I don't need your help! (*To the other women*) This is my husband's mother . . . couldn't provide a square meal, and says she wants to help me! I'm not going anywhere with you, and that's final!

GANGU. What's all the fuss about? Why don't you at least hear her out?

SANICHARI. Arre, I haven't come here to take her home . . . Actually, I've come here to help all of you . . . I'm here to offer you work as rudalis.

PARBATIA. I spit on your rudali work! Arre, you expect us to go and cry over the bodies of the very men who've ruined us!

SANICHARI. At least hear what I have to say, bahu . . .

PARBATIA. How dare you call me your bahu! I have a name—

Parbatia. I work as a whore and I'll continue in this line of work. I won't go off to cry over someone's dead body!

Parbatia exits.

GULBADAN. The old woman is crazy. Why the hell should we give up our regular income to go cry over some dead man?!

SANICHARI. Why not? You stand in line for a measly fifty paise. Arre, does this work of yours earn you enough to fill your stomach? Does it bring you self-respect? Ask her (*gestures towards Gangu*) did she get to eat two square meals yesterday? No clothes, no food, no self-respect . . .

CHAMPA. People don't die every day, do they? At least we work and earn every day.

GREYHAIRED WOMAN. Listen to her! As if there's a queue of clients lined up at her door!

CHAMPA. No, I won't go. This rudali work is too uncertain. There may be a job today, but what happens tomorrow?

SANICHARI. You're still young today—what happens tomorrow? Look, this is work, you hear me? Work. Better work than yours. Hard work like grinding grain in the chakki, splitting logs of wood, digging the earth . . .

SAEEDA. Any money in it?

SANICHARI. Yes, you make money, you get grain, clothes, the lot.

GANGU. Where do we have to go? Who's dead? Tell us that first . . .

SANICHARI. Gambhir Singh of Naugad.

GULBADAN. He's dead? Really?

SANICHARI. Yes, he passed away early this morning. His kriya will be held in grand style. Money and gifts will flow like water. Come, all of you come with me.

GREYHAIRED WOMAN. How much money will we make?

SANICHARI. Ten rupees a day, plus grain and clothes, and your meals as well.

GULBADAN. Whether anyone else goes or not, I'm definitely going. It's my father who's dead, you hear? My father! The

man who ruined me, who ruined my mother! How can I
not mourn at his funeral?

CHAMPA. Will we get coloured cloth?

SANICHARI. Not coloured, but definitely black cloth—

GANGU. Arre, you can sell it in the market and buy coloured
cloth instead.

They all come up and gather around Sanichari.

SAEEDA. He's no kith and kin of mine, though . . .

CHAMPA. Arre, so what! Come on; we'll arrange that as well!

GANGU. Hey, I've never done anything like this before, why
don't you show us how?

SANICHARI. When you start, weep as if you've lost someone
close to you, someone dear to your heart. Beat your breast
and cry out with such feeling that their blood runs cold!
Give it everything you have, make their hair stand on
end! (*She flings out her arms in demonstration, and lets out a loud,
mournful wail*) Hai re!

The rest of the women imitate her.

ALL. Hai re!

Blackout.

Scene 12

*A band is heard playing offstage. Hustle and bustle on stage. As the
lights come on, Gambhir Singh's corpse is seen lying on a cot, heaped
with flowers. Behind, some people are burning incense. To the left
chairs are arranged, on which the thakurs Lachman Singh, Madho
Singh, Nathuni Singh and their relatives are seated. Behind Lachman
Singh stands his armed bodyguard. The pandit is chanting shlokas
and sprinkling everyone with holy water. One of the zamindars is
laying a garland on the corpse. There is a strong stench emanating from
the body, which is affecting all those present. The zamindar covers his
face with a hanky and goes to sit beside the others. Gambhir Singh's
nephew and heir, Gajanan, is directing the arrangements. Madho
Singh is standing with him.*

PANDIT. Gambhir Singh took leave of this world at an
auspicious time, during the waxing phase of the moon. His
place in Paradise is assured.

LACHMAN SINGH. Panditji, a great soul like his is definitely
destined for Paradise. After all, he spent his whole life in
the service of our poorer brethren and the suffering
multitudes.

MADHO SINGH. Naugad has been orphaned today! Don't
distress yourself, Gajanan, we're all with you in your time
of trouble (*pats Gajanan on the back*).

BIJUA. Our master had a splendid life, and an even more
splendid death!

MAN. We're bereft at his passing. We've lost our main
support. (*Shouts*) Hey there! The incense has finished!
Bring fresh incense!

GAJANAN. Here, Lachman babu.

*He invites Lachman Singh to lay a garland on the corpse. Lachman
moves forward to do so. His gun-toting bodyguard follows him.
Madho Singh moves to stand behind the thakurs. A boy hands
Lachman Singh a garland. As he approaches the corpse, the stink of
decomposing flesh hits him. He flinches.*

LACHMAN SINGH. Gajanan, didn't you make arrangements to
sprinkle some attar or something? My brother was so fond
of perfumes! Go, someone, fetch four or five bottles of attar.
(*Handing his garland to the bodyguard*) Go on, you do it.

*Lachman Singh returns to his chair as his bodyguard places the
garland on the corpse. He too winces at the smell, holding his nose,
and then returns to his place. Meanwhile the band has stopped
playing.*

NATHUNI SINGH. Arre, Gajanan, why has the band stopped?

LACHMAN SINGH. Someone go and check. Have those bastards
been paid to sit still?

GAJANAN. Hey, Bhagirath, you go and see.

MADHO SINGH. Your inheritance papers are all in order, I
hope, Gajanan?

GAJANAN. Oh yes, that was all done while he was still alive.

My chacha was very generous.

Bhagirath comes running in. The sound of several voices raised in mourning can be heard offstage.

BHAGIRATH (*to Gajanan*). Malik, malik! A whole mob of rudalis is coming this way, crying at the top of their voices!

Bijua runs to the door with the incense burner in his hand. He peers out. There is an air of expectancy on stage. People start talking excitedly. Gajanan tries to calm them down. A crowd of rudalis enters, swathed in black from head to toe. They circle the corpse, wailing dramatically. Then they grasp the cot and sit down. Pairing off, they hold each other and sit down stage left, and begin to beat their foreheads and breasts rhythmically in exaggerated, stylized movements. They stand up, beating their breasts and wailing in unison, enjoying the rapt attention they are getting. They sing in unison.

RUDALIS. Hai re! Hai re!
  Hai, the master! Hai, father of us all!
  Hai, hai, smash all your bangles!
  Hai, hai, take off your toe-rings!
  Hai, hai, wipe off your alta!
  Hai, hai, wipe off your sindoor!
  Hai, hai, Naugad raja, hai, hai![1]

While this is going on, Gulbadan shrugs the black cloth off her head and deliberately holds Madho Singh's eyes. He responds by getting up and surreptitiously making his way to her. Lachman Singh notices this byplay and gets up, but then goes to the head of the corpse.

LACHMAN SINGH. Come on, come on, let's take the body out.

Madho Singh turns around. There is a stir on stage. The zamindars move forward to shoulder the body. Gajanan is amongst them. Some people begin to shower the corpse with khoi[2] and coins. They begin to chant 'Ram nam satya hai'.[3] The chant mingles with the wailing of the rudalis. Lachman Singh and the pandit lead the way, followed by the pall bearers, then the other people, with the wailing rudalis

---

1. Each of these is a social ritual of widowhood.
2. Khoi: parched/puffed rice.
-3. Literally, 'Ram is Truth!', a chant that accompanies the corpse to the cremation ground..

making up the rear. They move in procession across the stage. Sanichari is standing at stage left. Gulbadan slips out of the group of rudalis and goes up to Madho Singh, who is lingering behind the others. The two of them exchange a few words, then leave together. Sanichari looks at them, and then down at the edibles left lying about. The procession exits. Dulan comes on, carrying a bundle of foodstuffs, which he places beside the silent Sanichari.

DULAN. Here, take your stuff. Don't be late. I'm off. To the cremation ground. You'll get the money later.

Dulan exits. Sanichari lifts the bundle and slowly begins to make her way out. An incense burner is lying overturned. She straightens it. She sees a coin lying beside it. She picks it up. Looks at it. Smiles sadly. Knots it decisively into her clothing. Faces the audience resolutely. Blackout.

End.

Translated from the original Hindi.

Rudali
A Production Note

'Rudali' was first performed on 29 December 1992 at Sisir Manch, Calcutta, by Rangakarmee, with the following cast and crew:

Sanichari	*Usha Ganguli*
Bikhni	*Yama Shroff*
Parbatia	*Geetanjali Chugani*
Lachmi/Jugani	*Shreelekha Basu*
Thakurain/Jubaida	*Mallika Jalan*
Gangu/village woman	*Sheela Mishra*
Gulbadan/Saeeda	*Shubhra Choudhary*
Somri	*Afsari Begum*
Mishri/Naseeban	*Dipika Ganguli*
Dhatua's wife/Motia	*Ratna Roy*
Radhia/village women	*Lachmi Singh*
Champa	*Shabnam Vadhera*
village woman	*Ratna Roychoudhury*
village girl	*Deepa*
child Haroa	*Dipesh*
Dulan	*Om Pareek*
Lachman Singh	*Rajesh Sharma*
Madho Singh	*Narendra Roy*

Pandit/sweetseller/villager	*S.K.Tiwari*
Bachanlal/vaid	*J.P.Singh*
Bijua	*Chhavilal*
Budhua/Bikhni's nephew/ bodyguard	*Ajay Yadav*
Natua	*Manoj Choudhary*
Bachha Singh/Gajanan	*Debu Shome*
Sankar	*Tarak Chatterjee*
Bhairo Singh	*Bhaskar Mitra*
Villager	*Ratan Dey*
Gambhir Singh	*Rajesh Rao*
Haroa/village boy	*Dilip Bharti*

Direction, script, set, music, costumes	*Usha Ganguli*
Assistants	*Rajesh Sharma, Narendra Roy*
Light design	*Badal Das*
Light operation	*Lakhan Ghosh, Sashanka Ghosh Bhondal Dass*
Set-in-charge	*Rajesh Sharma*
Assistants	*Bhasan Chandan*
Properties in-charge	*Debu Shome*
Assistants	*Monoj Choudhury*
Costumes-in-charge	*Dilip Bharti*
Stage Manager	*Narendra Roy*
Makeup-in-charge	*Ajay Yadav*

The final Hindi script of Rudali *was written by Usha Ganguli after a workshop exercise in which an initial Bengali script was evolved. Participants in the workshop included three playwrights, Partha Banerjee, Subir Mukherjee and Samar Chatterjee; consultant Samik Bandyopadhyay; Usha Ganguli and Rangakarmee member Narendra Roy. The inputs of the playwrights of the workshop script are gratefully acknowledged.*